FOR CHOCOLATE LOVERS

Ottenheimer Publishers, Inc.

Managing Editor: Diane B. Anderson
Associate Editor: Elaine Christiansen
Senior Food Editor: Jackie Sheehan
Test Kitchen Coordinator: Pat Peterson
Circulation Specialist: Karen Goodsell
Food Editor and Food Stylist's Assistant: Bonnie Ellingboe
Food Stylist: Barb Standal
Contributing Editor: Patricia Miller
Home Economists: Pillsbury Publications
Nutrition Coordinator: Patricia Godfrey, R.D.
Design, Production: Tad Ware & Company, Inc.
Photography: Studio 3

**This edition published by arrangement
with Ottenheimer Publishers, Inc.,
distributed by Wholesale Warehousing Industries, Inc.,
250 Granton Drive, Richmond Hill, Ontario, Canada, L4B 1H7.**

Cover Photo: Black Forest Tart p. 21, Chocolate Filigree Heart p. 47

Black Forest Tart p. 21, Chocolate Filigree Heart p. 47

CONTENTS

CHOCOLATE? YES!

Aficionados and just plain fans alike say "yes" to the magical allure of chocolate.

Double Chocolate Chunk Cupcakes p. 63

Centuries ago, deep in the impenetrable jungles of the Amazon, the Mayans discovered a fragile evergreen adorned with delicate white flowers, and ripening pods of flaming red, yellow, and brilliant green. From the seeds of the ripe pods, they concocted a bitter beverage they called xocoatl or chocolatl. And the rest, is history.

From the halls of Montezuma, Cortes carried cocoa beans and the beverage made from them to the court of Emperor Charles V. For 300 years, chocolate remained a gritty, bitter drink that monks, nuns and chemists sought to improve by thickening it with corn meal and starches and seasoning it with spices.

In 1828, a Dutch chemist invented the technique for producing cocoa powder and cocoa butter—the base for the melt-in-your-mouth appeal of modern chocolate. By adding sugar and vanilla to the creamy cocoa butter, chocolate as we know it was born. Nearly a quarter of a century later, the first chocolate bar was tasted.

The love of chocolate began thousands of years ago among the civilizations of Central and South America. Through the centuries chocolate gained enthusiasts from the throne rooms of Europe to the cities of the New World. It was credited with medicinal benefits, and the courtesans of 17th and 18th century Europe claimed it was an aphrodisiac.

Chocolate's allure has not diminished or died, but has grown and flourished in every society it is introduced. Why? Plain and simple, the taste. Its many-splendoured flavors shade from the bite of extra bittersweet to the mellowness of Swiss milk chocolate.

For those of us captured in the web of chocolate's intrigue, too much is never enough. We indulge in rich, gooey confections. We bite into bonbons. We snack on chips and bars of chocolate. By choice we select concoctions of chocolate and its complementary cousins such as peanut butter, caramel, mint, coffee and vanilla. And by comparison, non-chocolate sweets seem pale, uninteresting, flavorless and a poor second choice.

2

Chocolate — Varieties and Forms

Today's myriad varieties and forms of chocolate turn supermarkets into paradise for chocolate lovers.

Unsweetened chocolate — is the basic chocolate from which all other products are made. It is molded into 1-ounce blocks and packed eight to a carton. Unsweetened chocolate is the base for most brownies, cakes, frostings and dark chocolate candies.

Semi-sweet chocolate — is unsweetened chocolate with sugar, additional cocoa butter and flavorings added. Molded into 1-ounce blocks and packed eight to a carton or formed into chocolate chips ranging in size from mini to large "gourmet" to chunks, it is sold in 6-, 12- or 24-ounce packages. Semi-sweet chocolate is versatile and used in desserts, cookies, bars, fillings and candies.

Sweet cooking chocolate — also called German sweet chocolate, it is similar to semi-sweet chocolate but with a higher proportion of sugar. It is packed in 4-ounce bars. Sweet chocolate is especially flavorful in cakes and as filling for Danish pastries.

Milk chocolate — is sweet chocolate with milk added and is packaged in various size bars and shapes. Candy bars are the most common form of milk chocolate, but it also is used in cookies, bars and desserts.

Unsweetened cocoa — is pure chocolate with most of the cocoa butter removed and ground into powder form. It is available in 8- or 16-ounce cans. Cocoa is commonly used in beverages, sauces and baking.

Chocolate-flavored syrup — is a combination of cocoa, corn syrup and flavoring. Available in various size jars or cans, it is most often used to make chocolate beverages and as a dessert topping.

White chocolate — one of the most popular products, is not really chocolate but a combination of cocoa butter, sugar, milk and flavorings. It is available in 6-oz. bars, regular-sized chips and large "gourmet" chips. Almond bark, also known as vanilla-flavored candy coating, is sold in packages divided into 1 to 2 ounce squares. White chocolate is used in cookies, candies, desserts and frostings. Due to variations among white chocolate products, use specific products called for in the recipe.

Imitation chocolate — contains no cocoa butter and can sacrifice flavor and performance. This product is usually referred to as chocolate-flavored.

Chocolate Substitutions

Throughout this book, each recipe will specify which form of chocolate performs best. In a pinch, different chocolate products can be substituted. The flavors may vary, but to a chocolate lover, variety is the spice of life!

- For semi-sweet chocolate chips in cookie recipes, substitute white or milk chocolate chips or chunks.

- For 1 ounce (1 square) unsweetened chocolate, use 3 tablespoons unsweetened cocoa and 1 tablespoon shortening or oil.

- For 1 ounce (1 square) semi-sweet chocolate, use 3 tablespoons semi-sweet chocolate chips or 1 ounce unsweetened chocolate and 1 tablespoon sugar.

- For 6 ounces (1 cup) semi-sweet chocolate chips to be melted, use 6 tablespoons unsweetened cocoa, ¼ cup sugar and ¼ cup shortening.

- For a 4-ounce bar of sweet cooking chocolate to be melted, use ¼ cup unsweetened cocoa, ⅓ cup sugar and 3 tablespoons shortening.

SPECTACULAR DESSERTS

*Don't be surprised when
your guests give you a
standing ovation!*

♡

When you want to knock their socks
off. When you want them to stand up
and cheer. When nothing but the best
will do. **That's** when you serve a
spectacular dessert. And this
selection of desserts is nothing short
of spectacular.

But don't let the vision of fireworks,
the crash of cymbals or the fanfare of
trumpets deter you from attempting
these tempting creations. Although
some are elaborate and elegant,
they're not too difficult. They've been
written with you in mind, tested and
re-tested, tasted and re-tasted to
ensure that your success is our
success.

We've included some tricks of the
trade, too. Like how to make
chocolate curls and chocolate filigree
hearts—garnishes that rival those
found in the ritziest restaurants. On
the subject of garnishes, it's the sprig
of mint, the piping of whipped
cream, the dusting of confectioner's
sugar, or the ripe red strawberry
placed just right that turns ordinary
into extraordinary.

So set aside some special cooking
time, dust off your china, crystal or
silver serving pieces, and prepare
yourself for a standing ovation.

*Triple Chocolate Cake p. 6, Chocolate-
Dipped Strawberries p. 41, Large Chocolate
Curls p. 45*

This cake is a unique combination of varied chocolate intensities. It makes a perfect birthday cake for the true chocolate lover.

TRIPLE CHOCOLATE CAKE

CAKE
1 pkg. Pillsbury Plus Devil's Food Cake Mix
1 cup dairy sour cream
¾ cup water
⅓ cup oil
3 eggs
4-oz. bar milk chocolate, chopped

FROSTING
8 oz. white baking bar, cut into pieces
¾ cup butter or margarine, softened
½ cup powdered sugar

Heat oven to 350°F. Grease and flour two 9-inch round cake pans. In large bowl, combine cake mix, sour cream, water, oil and eggs at low speed until moistened; beat 2 minutes at high speed. Gently fold in milk chocolate. Pour batter evenly into greased and floured pans. Bake at 350°F. for 30 to 40 minutes or until cake springs back when touched lightly in center. Cool 15 minutes; remove from pans. Cool completely.

Melt white baking bar in small saucepan over low heat, stirring constantly. Remove from heat; cool. In small bowl, beat butter and powdered sugar until fluffy. Gradually beat in cooled baking bar until smooth and fluffy. To assemble cake, place 1 layer bottom side up on serving plate. Spread ½ cup frosting over layer. Place remaining layer bottom side down on frosted layer. Frost sides and top of cake with remaining frosting. Garnish as desired. 16 servings.

HIGH ALTITUDE—Above 3500 Feet: Add ¼ cup flour to dry cake mix.
Bake as directed above.

NUTRITION INFORMATION PER SERVING

SERVING SIZE: 1/16 OF RECIPE		PERCENT U.S. RDA PER SERVING	
CALORIES	430	PROTEIN	6%
PROTEIN	5g	VITAMIN A	10%
CARBOHYDRATE	41g	VITAMIN C	*
FAT	27g	THIAMINE	4%
CHOLESTEROL	90mg	RIBOFLAVIN	8%
SODIUM	370mg	NIACIN	2%
POTASSIUM	230mg	CALCIUM	15%
		IRON	4%

*Contains less than 2% of the U.S. RDA of this nutrient.

Crisp rice cereal and nuts are folded into fudge frosting to make the crust for this sherbet pie. Miniature chocolate chips would make an ideal topping.

FUDGY SHERBET PIE

1 cup crisp rice cereal
½ cup chopped nuts
1 can Pillsbury Frosting Supreme Ready To Spread Chocolate Fudge Frosting
1 quart (4 cups) orange sherbet, softened

Brush 9-inch pie pan with oil. In large bowl, combine cereal, nuts and frosting until cereal is well coated. Press mixture in bottom and up sides of oiled pan. Freeze until slightly firm, about 30 minutes. Spread sherbet in crust. Cover; freeze until firm. 8 servings.

NUTRITION INFORMATION PER SERVING

SERVING SIZE: 1/8 OF RECIPE		PERCENT U.S. RDA PER SERVING	
CALORIES	430	PROTEIN	4%
PROTEIN	3g	VITAMIN A	4%
CARBOHYDRATE	69g	VITAMIN C	6%
FAT	16g	THIAMINE	6%
CHOLESTEROL	6mg	RIBOFLAVIN	6%
SODIUM	210mg	NIACIN	4%
POTASSIUM	280mg	CALCIUM	6%
		IRON	6%

This is a traditional cheesecake baked in a chocolate cookie crumb crust. Drizzle the chocolate glaze in a fancy design for a special finishing touch.

CHOCOLATE CHIP CHEESECAKE

CRUST
- 2 cups crushed creme-filled chocolate sandwich cookies
- 2 tablespoons margarine or butter, melted

FILLING
- 3 eggs
- 2 (8-oz.) pkg. cream cheese, softened
- ¾ cup sugar
- 1 teaspoon vanilla
- ½ cup whipping cream
- 1 cup miniature semi-sweet chocolate chips

GLAZE
- ¼ cup miniature semi-sweet chocolate chips
- 1 teaspoon shortening

Heat oven to 325°F. In medium bowl, combine crust ingredients; press in bottom and 1 inch up sides of 10-inch springform pan.

Beat eggs in large bowl. Add cream cheese, sugar and vanilla; beat until smooth. Add whipping cream; blend well. Stir in 1 cup chocolate chips. Pour into crust-lined pan. Bake at 325°F. for 60 to 75 minutes or until center is set. (To minimize cracking, place shallow pan half full of hot water on lower oven rack during baking.) Cool.

In small saucepan, melt ¼ cup chocolate chips with shortening over low heat, stirring constantly. Drizzle over cooled cheesecake. Refrigerate several hours or overnight. Before serving, carefully remove sides of pan. 12 servings.

NUTRITION INFORMATION PER SERVING

SERVING SIZE: 1/12 OF RECIPE		PERCENT U.S. RDA PER SERVING	
CALORIES	450	PROTEIN	10%
PROTEIN	6g	VITAMIN A	15%
CARBOHYDRATE	36g	VITAMIN C	*
FAT	31g	THIAMINE	4%
CHOLESTEROL	130mg	RIBOFLAVIN	10%
SODIUM	240mg	NIACIN	2%
POTASSIUM	135mg	CALCIUM	4%
		IRON	8%

*Contains less than 2% of the U.S. RDA of this nutrient.

This is a perfect dessert to have ready and waiting for a larger group. It refrigerates well overnight and serves 12 to 16.

FRUITED CHOCOLATE TRIFLE

- 9-inch baked chocolate or yellow cake layer
- 1½ cups cold milk
- 4-oz. pkg. chocolate instant pudding or pie filling mix
- 2 cups whipping cream, whipped
- 2 cups sliced fresh strawberries
- 2 medium ripe bananas, sliced*
- 1 tablespoon sliced almonds
  Strawberries, if desired

Cut cake into 1-inch cubes; set aside. In small bowl, combine milk and pudding mix; beat at low speed 1 to 2 minutes. Let stand 5 minutes to thicken. Fold 1½ cups of the whipped cream into pudding. Spoon about ⅓ of the pudding mixture into bottom of 2½-quart straight-sided glass serving bowl. Add ⅓ of the fruits and ⅓ of the cake cubes. Repeat layers two more times, forming 3 layers of pudding, fruit and cake. Pipe or dollop remaining whipped cream over top layer of cake cubes. Garnish with sliced almonds and strawberries. Store in refrigerator. 12 to 16 servings.

TIP: *To prevent bananas from browning, dip in orange juice and drain prior to assembling trifle.

NUTRITION INFORMATION PER SERVING

SERVING SIZE: 1/16 OF RECIPE		PERCENT U.S. RDA PER SERVING	
CALORIES	280	PROTEIN	4%
PROTEIN	3g	VITAMIN A	10%
CARBOHYDRATE	29g	VITAMIN C	35%
FAT	17g	THIAMINE	4%
CHOLESTEROL	60mg	RIBOFLAVIN	8%
SODIUM	135mg	NIACIN	2%
POTASSIUM	220mg	CALCIUM	8%
		IRON	4%

Heat oven to 450°F. Prepare pie crust according to package directions for **unfilled one-crust pie** using 9-inch pie pan. (Refrigerate remaining crust for later use.) Bake at 450°F. for 9 to 11 minutes or until light golden brown. Cool completely.

This is a simplified and lighter version of an all-time favorite chocolate pie. All Ready Pie Crusts help make the preparation a snap.

CREAMY FRENCH SILK PIE

15-oz. pkg. Pillsbury All Ready Pie
    Crusts
  1 teaspoon flour

FILLING
  ¼ cup sugar
  3 tablespoons cornstarch
1½ cups milk
6-oz. pkg. (1 cup) semi-sweet
    chocolate chips
  1 teaspoon vanilla
1½ cups whipping cream
  2 tablespoons powdered sugar

In medium saucepan, combine sugar and cornstarch; blend well. Gradually add milk; cook over medium heat until mixture boils, stirring constantly. Reserve one tablespoon chocolate chips for topping. Add remaining chocolate chips and vanilla, stirring until melted and smooth. Pour into large mixing bowl; cover surface with plastic wrap. Cool to room temperature.

In large bowl, combine whipping cream and powdered sugar; beat until soft peaks form. Reserve 1½ cups for topping. Beat cooled chocolate mixture at medium speed until light and fluffy, about 1 minute; fold chocolate mixture into whipped cream. Spoon evenly into cooled crust. Top with reserved whipped cream. Chop reserved chocolate chips; sprinkle over top. Refrigerate 2 to 3 hours before serving. Refrigerate any remaining dessert. 10 servings.

NUTRITION INFORMATION PER SERVING

SERVING SIZE: 1/10 OF RECIPE		PERCENT U.S. RDA PER SERVING	
CALORIES	370	PROTEIN	4%
PROTEIN	3g	VITAMIN A	10%
CARBOHYDRATE	31g	VITAMIN C	*
FAT	26g	THIAMINE	*
CHOLESTEROL	60mg	RIBOFLAVIN	6%
SODIUM	115mg	NIACIN	*
POTASSIUM	150mg	CALCIUM	6%
		IRON	2%

*Contains less than 2% of the U.S. RDA of this nutrient.

Creamy French Silk Pie

This is the ultimate chocolate dessert!

CHOCOLATE CHEESECAKE

CRUST
8½-oz. pkg. chocolate wafers, crushed (1¾ cups)
6 tablespoons margarine or butter, melted

FILLING
2 (8-oz.) pkg. cream cheese, softened
⅔ cup sugar
3 eggs
12-oz. pkg. (2 cups) semi-sweet chocolate chips, melted
1 cup whipping cream
2 tablespoons margarine or butter, melted
1 teaspoon vanilla

Heat oven to 325°F. In medium bowl, combine crust ingredients; reserve 1 tablespoon crumbs for garnish. Press remaining crumbs over bottom and 2 inches up sides of 10-inch springform pan. Refrigerate.

In large bowl, combine cream cheese and sugar; beat until smooth. Add eggs, one at a time, beating after each addition until well blended. Add melted chocolate; beat well. Add whipping cream, 2 tablespoons margarine and vanilla; beat until smooth. Pour into crust-lined pan.

Bake at 325°F. for 55 to 65 minutes or until edges are set. Center of cheesecake will be soft. (To minimize cracking, place shallow pan half full of hot water on lower oven rack during baking.) Cool in pan 5 minutes; carefully remove sides of pan. Cool. Garnish with reserved crumbs. Refrigerate several hours or overnight before serving. 16 servings.

NUTRITION INFORMATION PER SERVING

SERVING SIZE: 1/16 OF RECIPE		PERCENT U.S. RDA PER SERVING	
CALORIES	440	PROTEIN	8%
PROTEIN	6g	VITAMIN A	20%
CARBOHYDRATE	33g	VITAMIN C	*
FAT	32g	THIAMINE	4%
CHOLESTEROL	110mg	RIBOFLAVIN	8%
SODIUM	190mg	NIACIN	2%
POTASSIUM	150mg	CALCIUM	4%
		IRON	8%

*Contains less than 2% of the U.S. RDA of this nutrient.

An eye-catching dessert everyone will love made conveniently with pancake mix.

BLACK FOREST DESSERT CREPES

FILLING
2½ cups half-and-half
3½-oz. pkg. instant vanilla pudding and pie filling mix
1 egg, separated, reserving yolk for crepes
2 tablespoons sugar
2 tablespoons almond-flavored liqueur

CREPES
1 cup Hungry Jack® Extra Lights® Complete or Buttermilk Complete Pancake Mix
2 tablespoons sugar
2 tablespoons unsweetened cocoa
1¼ cups water
2 tablespoons margarine or butter, melted
2 eggs
Reserved egg yolk

TOPPING
21-oz. can cherry fruit pie filling, chilled

In large bowl, combine half-and-half and pudding mix; beat 2 minutes at low speed or until well blended. Let stand until set, about 5 minutes. In small bowl, beat egg white until foamy. Gradually add 2 tablespoons sugar; beat until stiff peaks form. Fold into pudding mixture. Stir in liqueur. Refrigerate while preparing crepes.

In small bowl, combine pancake mix, 2 tablespoons sugar and cocoa. Add water, margarine, 2 eggs and egg yolk; beat until batter is smooth. Heat crepe pan or small skillet over medium heat; grease lightly with oil. Pour scant ¼ cup batter into hot skillet, immediately tilting pan until batter covers bottom. Cook until edges start to dry and center is set. If desired, turn to brown other side. Cool.

To serve, spoon 2 tablespoons filling onto each crepe; roll up gently. Place 2 crepes on each serving plate. Top with scant ¼ cup pie filling. Serve immediately. 8 to 10 servings.

TIP: To make crepes ahead, prepare, wrap well in foil and store in refrigerator up to 3 days or freezer up to 3 months. To thaw, place package in 300°F. oven for 10 to 15 minutes.

HIGH ALTITUDE—Above 3500 Feet: No change.

Miniature chocolate chips boost the flavor of this chocolate cake. A rum syrup creates a wonderfully moist and tender texture.

FUDGY RUM CAKE

CAKE
1 pkg. Pillsbury Plus Devil's Food Cake Mix
1 cup water
½ cup dairy sour cream
3 eggs
½ cup miniature semi-sweet chocolate chips

SYRUP
2 tablespoons sugar
¼ cup water
¼ cup dark rum*

GLAZE
¼ cup miniature semi-sweet chocolate chips
1 tablespoon whipping cream
1 tablespoon light corn syrup

Heat oven to 350°F. Generously grease and flour 12-cup fluted tube pan. In large bowl, combine cake mix, 1 cup water, sour cream and eggs. Beat at low speed until moistened; beat 2 minutes at highest speed. Stir in ½ cup chocolate chips. Pour into greased and floured pan. Bake at 350°F. for 45 to 50 minutes or until toothpick inserted in center comes out clean. Cool upright in pan 10 minutes.

Meanwhile, in small saucepan combine all syrup ingredients. Bring to a boil, stirring until sugar is dissolved. Cool 5 minutes. Randomly prick entire top of cake with long-tined fork. Slowly pour warm syrup over cake. Remove cake from pan after syrup has been absorbed, about 15 minutes; cool.

In small saucepan, combine all glaze ingredients; heat over medium-low heat until melted, stirring constantly. Spoon evenly over cooled cake. 12 to 16 servings.

TIP: *Two teaspoons rum extract and enough water to make ¼ cup can be substituted for dark rum.

HIGH ALTITUDE—Above 3500 Feet: Add ¼ cup flour to dry cake mix. Increase water in cake to 1⅓ cups. Bake as directed above.

Our taste panel enthusiastically put its stamp of approval on this recipe. A refreshing white chocolate mousse is served in a pool of luscious raspberry sauce. Both can be made early in the day for relaxed assembly just before serving.

WHITE CHOCOLATE MOUSSE DE RASPBERRY

SAUCE

10-oz. pkg. frozen raspberries with syrup, thawed
2 tablespoons sugar
1 tablespoon frozen orange juice concentrate

MOUSSE

2 cups whipping cream
6-oz. pkg. white baking bar, cut into pieces
1 teaspoon vanilla

GLAZE

¼ cup milk chocolate chips
1 teaspoon oil

In blender container or food processor bowl with metal blade, combine all sauce ingredients. Process until smooth; strain to remove seeds. Refrigerate.

In medium saucepan, melt whipping cream and white baking bar over low heat, stirring constantly until smooth. Stir in vanilla. Pour into large bowl; cover with plastic wrap. Refrigerate 6 hours or overnight until mixture is **very cold and thickened**, stirring occasionally. Using mixer, beat cream mixture at high speed until light and fluffy. DO NOT OVERBEAT.

Melt glaze ingredients in small saucepan over very low heat until smooth, stirring constantly. To serve, pour scant ¼ cup raspberry sauce onto each dessert plate. Spoon ½ cup mousse in center of plate. Drizzle glaze over mousse and sauce. Garnish as desired. 6 servings.

NUTRITION INFORMATION PER SERVING

SERVING SIZE: 1/6 OF RECIPE		PERCENT U.S. RDA PER SERVING	
CALORIES	540	PROTEIN	6%
PROTEIN	4g	VITAMIN A	25%
CARBOHYDRATE	41g	VITAMIN C	20%
FAT	41g	THIAMINE	2%
CHOLESTEROL	116mg	RIBOFLAVIN	10%
SODIUM	60mg	NIACIN	*
POTASSIUM	250mg	CALCIUM	10%
		IRON	2%

*Contains less than 2% of the U.S. RDA of this nutrient.

White Chocolate Mousse De Raspberry

This is a wonderfully light and refreshing fruit dessert to serve after a big meal. It's sure to please chocolate lovers, too.

CHOCO-CARAMEL DRIZZLED ORANGES

4 medium seedless oranges
¼ cup margarine or butter
¾ cup firmly packed brown sugar
1 tablespoon light corn syrup
¼ cup milk
¼ cup semi-sweet chocolate chips
¼ cup chopped pecans

Peel oranges; remove white membrane. Slice each orange into 4 or 5 round slices; set aside. Melt margarine in small saucepan. Add brown sugar and corn syrup; bring to a boil, stirring constantly until sugar is dissolved. Gradually add milk to boiling caramel mixture, stirring constantly; remove from heat. Pour ½ cup caramel mixture into glass measuring cup. To remaining caramel mixture add chocolate chips; stir until melted.

Arrange orange slices on 4 serving plates. Drizzle each serving with 2 tablespoons caramel mixture and 3 tablespoons chocolate-caramel mixture. Sprinkle each with 1 tablespoon pecans. 4 servings.

▥ MICROWAVE DIRECTIONS:
Prepare orange slices as directed above. In 4-cup microwave-safe measuring cup or small bowl, combine margarine, brown sugar and corn syrup. Microwave on HIGH for 1 to 2 minutes or until mixture boils and sugar is dissolved, stirring once halfway through cooking. Whisk in milk. Microwave on MEDIUM for 1 to 2 minutes or until mixtures boils, stirring once halfway through cooking. Pour ½ cup caramel mixture into bowl. To remaining caramel mixture add chocolate chips; stir until melted. Serve as directed above.

NUTRITION INFORMATION PER SERVING

SERVING SIZE: 1/4 OF RECIPE		PERCENT U.S. RDA PER SERVING	
CALORIES	460	PROTEIN	4%
PROTEIN	3g	VITAMIN A	15%
CARBOHYDRATE	68g	VITAMIN C	120%
FAT	20g	THIAMINE	10%
CHOLESTEROL	0mg	RIBOFLAVIN	6%
SODIUM	160mg	NIACIN	2%
POTASSIUM	470mg	CALCIUM	10%
		IRON	10%

A thin slice of this layered dessert is sure to satisfy your sweet tooth. Salted peanuts in the crust and topping add a special flavor to complement the chocolate.

CHOCO-PEANUT MOUSSE PIE

CRUST
1½ cups crushed shortbread cookies
⅓ cup finely chopped salted peanuts
¼ cup margarine or butter, melted
2 tablespoons sugar

CHOCOLATE LAYER
8 oz. (1⅓ cups) semi-sweet chocolate chips
1 cup hot milk

PEANUT BUTTER LAYER
6 oz. (1 cup) peanut butter chips
½ cup hot milk
1 cup whipping cream, whipped
2 tablespoons powdered sugar
⅓ cup chopped salted peanuts

Heat oven to 350°F. In medium bowl, combine all crust ingredients; mix well. Press in bottom and 1½ inches up sides of 9-inch springform pan. Bake at 350°F. for 9 to 11 minutes or until light golden brown. Cool completely.

In blender container or food processor bowl with metal blade, combine chocolate chips and 1 cup hot milk. Cover; blend until smooth. Pour into small bowl; cover with plastic wrap. In blender container or food processor bowl with metal blade, combine peanut butter chips and ½ cup hot milk. Cover; blend until smooth. Pour mixture into large bowl; cover with plastic wrap. Refrigerate chocolate mixture and peanut butter mixture 1 hour or until slightly thickened.

Spread chocolate mixture in cooled crust. Fold whipped cream and powdered sugar into peanut butter mixture; spread evenly over chocolate layer. Sprinkle with ⅓ cup chopped peanuts. Refrigerate until firm. Refrigerate any remaining dessert. 12 servings.

NUTRITION INFORMATION PER SERVING

SERVING SIZE:		PERCENT U.S. RDA	
1/12 OF RECIPE		PER SERVING	
CALORIES	430	PROTEIN	10%
PROTEIN	8g	VITAMIN A	10%
CARBOHYDRATE	33g	VITAMIN C	*
FAT	30g	THIAMINE	8%
CHOLESTEROL	35mg	RIBOFLAVIN	8%
SODIUM	180mg	NIACIN	15%
POTASSIUM	260mg	CALCIUM	8%
		IRON	6%

*Contains less than 2% of the U.S. RDA of this nutrient.

This dessert has a chocolate wafer base topped with a mint-flavored cheesecake and frosted with rich semi-sweet chocolate. The 13x9-inch pan makes enough to serve 20 guests.

CREME DE MENTHE CHEESECAKE SQUARES

CRUST
- 8½-oz. pkg. chocolate wafers, crushed (1¾ cups)
- ½ cup margarine or butter, melted

FILLING
- 2 (8-oz.) pkg. cream cheese, softened
- ½ cup dairy sour cream
- 4 eggs
- ⅔ cup sugar
- ½ cup creme de menthe syrup
- ¼ teaspoon mint extract

TOPPING
- 4 oz. (4 squares) semi-sweet chocolate, cut into pieces
- ½ cup dairy sour cream

Heat oven to 350°F. In medium bowl, combine crust ingredients; press in bottom and 1 inch up sides of ungreased 13x9-inch pan. Freeze crust while preparing filling.

In large bowl, combine all filling ingredients; beat on low speed until smooth. Pour into crust-lined pan. Bake at 350°F. for 30 to 35 minutes or until knife inserted in center comes out clean. Cool on wire rack.

Melt chocolate in small saucepan over low heat, stirring constantly. Cool 5 minutes; whisk or beat in sour cream. Spread over warm cheesecake. Refrigerate 3 hours or until firm. Cut into squares. 20 servings.

NUTRITION INFORMATION PER SERVING

SERVING SIZE:		PERCENT U.S. RDA	
1/20 OF RECIPE		PER SERVING	
CALORIES	300	PROTEIN	6%
PROTEIN	4g	VITAMIN A	15%
CARBOHYDRATE	23g	VITAMIN C	*
FAT	20g	THIAMINE	2%
CHOLESTEROL	90mg	RIBOFLAVIN	8%
SODIUM	160mg	NIACIN	*
POTASSIUM	95mg	CALCIUM	4%
		IRON	6%

*Contains less than 2% of the U.S. RDA of this nutrient.

COOK'S NOTE
CHOCOLATE THAT THICKENS OR "SEIZES" DURING MELTING

Small amounts of unwanted moisture can cause chocolate to become thick, lumpy and grainy during melting. "Seizing" is caused by condensation of steam droplets when heat is too high or when water is on utensils.

Often chocolate can be brought back to a melted consistency by adding 1 teaspoon solid shortening for every 2 ounces of chocolate and reheating.

Dip tumbler bottoms in melted chocolat candy coating to create individual dessert cups. Fill each cup with fluffy white chocolate mousse and top with seasonal fresh fruits.

FRUIT AND CREAM TIMBALE CUPS

6 (6-inch) squares cut from foil
6 glass or plastic tumblers, 2 to 2¼ inches at base
8 oz. chocolate-flavored candy coating, cut into pieces
1 cup whipping cream
3 oz. (3 squares) white baking bar, cut into pieces
1 cup sliced fresh fruit*

Center tumbler bases on foil squares and cover tightly. Melt chocolate in small saucepan over low heat, stirring constantly. Dip foil-wrapped tumblers in chocolate to depth of 1 inch; allow excess to drip back into melted chocolate. Place tumblers, chocolate side up, on tray; refrigerate until set. If necessary, heat chocolate as directed above and dip again. Refrigerate until set. Remove chocolate-coated foil from tumbler; carefully remove foil from chocolate.

In small saucepan, combine cream and white baking bar; melt over low heat until smooth, stirring constantly. Refrigerate mixture about 3 hours or until very cold and thickened, stirring occasionally. Using mixer, beat cream mixture at high speed until stiff. Spoon about ⅓ cup cream mixture into each chocolate cup; top with 2 tablespoons fruit. Serve immediately. 6 servings.

TIP: *Use strawberries, peaches, kiwifruit, bananas, seedless grapes, blueberries, raspberries or other desired fruit.

NUTRITION INFORMATION PER SERVING

SERVING SIZE: 1/6 OF RECIPE		PERCENT U.S. RDA PER SERVING	
CALORIES	450	PROTEIN	4%
PROTEIN	3g	VITAMIN A	10%
CARBOHYDRATE	33g	VITAMIN C	40%
FAT	34g	THIAMINE	25%
CHOLESTEROL	60mg	RIBOFLAVIN	30%
SODIUM	55mg	NIACIN	2%
POTASSIUM	210mg	CALCIUM	10%
		IRON	*

*Contains less than 2% of the U.S. RDA of this nutrient.

Fruit And Cream Timbale Cup

Heat oven to 350°F. Grease bottom only of 13x9-inch pan. In large bowl, combine all brownie ingredients; beat 50 strokes with spoon. Spread in greased pan. Bake at 350°F. for 33 to 35 minutes or until set. DO NOT OVERBAKE. Cool completely.

That all-time favorite banana split is now made with a brownie crust. What more could you want!

BANANA SPLIT BROWNIE DESSERT

BROWNIES
21½-oz. pkg. Pillsbury Fudge
        Brownie Mix
    ½ cup water
    ½ cup oil
    2 eggs

TOPPING
    3 medium-sized ripe bananas,
        thinly sliced
    ½ gallon (8 cups) vanilla ice
        cream, softened
12-oz. jar strawberry ice cream
        topping
12-oz. jar pineapple ice cream
        topping
        Sweetened whipped cream,
        if desired
        Chopped nuts, if desired
        Maraschino cherries, if
        desired

Arrange sliced bananas over cooled brownies. Spoon ice cream over bananas; gently spread to evenly cover bananas. Cover; freeze until firm, about 8 hours or overnight. To serve, let stand at room temperature about 15 minutes; cut into squares. Spoon about 1 tablespoon each of strawberry and pineapple ice cream toppings over each serving. Top each with whipped cream, chopped nuts and a cherry.
20 to 24 servings.

HIGH ALTITUDE—Above 3500 Feet: Add ¼ cup flour to dry brownie mix. Bake as directed above.

NUTRITION INFORMATION PER SERVING

SERVING SIZE: 1 BROWNIE		PERCENT U.S. RDA PER SERVING	
CALORIES	390	PROTEIN	6%
PROTEIN	4g	VITAMIN A	6%
CARBOHYDRATE	59g	VITAMIN C	8%
FAT	16g	THIAMINE	6%
CHOLESTEROL	50mg	RIBOFLAVIN	10%
SODIUM	140mg	NIACIN	2%
POTASSIUM	240mg	CALCIUM	8%
		IRON	4%

Keep this frozen dessert on hand for unexpected guests. For easier serving, allow it to thaw in the refrigerator for 15 to 20 minutes before cutting.

CREAMY MOCHA FROZEN DESSERT

CRUST

> 1 cup chocolate wafer cookie crumbs (about 18)
> ½ cup finely chopped pecans
> ¼ cup margarine or butter, melted

FILLING

> 2 (8-oz.) pkg. cream cheese, softened
> 14-oz. can sweetened condensed milk (not evaporated)
> ½ cup chocolate-flavored syrup
> 2 teaspoons instant coffee granules or crystals
> 1 tablespoon water
> 8-oz. container frozen whipped topping, thawed
> ¼ cup chopped pecans

In medium bowl, combine all crust ingredients; blend well. Press firmly in bottom of 13x9-inch pan or 10-inch springform pan.

In large bowl, beat cream cheese until fluffy. Beat in sweetened condensed milk and chocolate syrup until smooth. In small bowl, combine instant coffee and water; stir until dissolved. Stir into cream cheese mixture. Fold in whipped topping; spoon into crust-lined pan. Sprinkle evenly with ¼ cup pecans. Freeze overnight or until firm. 16 servings.

NUTRITION INFORMATION PER SERVING

SERVING SIZE: 1/16 OF RECIPE		PERCENT U.S. RDA PER SERVING	
CALORIES	370	PROTEIN	8%
PROTEIN	6g	VITAMIN A	15%
CARBOHYDRATE	34g	VITAMIN C	*
FAT	24g	THIAMINE	4%
CHOLESTEROL	45mg	RIBOFLAVIN	10%
SODIUM	180mg	NIACIN	*
POTASSIUM	220mg	CALCIUM	10%
		IRON	4%

*Contains less than 2% of the U.S. RDA of this nutrient.

An old-fashioned dessert the whole family will love. It makes its own fudge sauce.

HOT FUDGE PUDDING CAKE

> 1¼ cups Pillsbury's BEST® All Purpose or Unbleached Flour
> ¾ cup sugar
> 2 tablespoons unsweetened cocoa
> 1½ teaspoons baking powder
> ½ teaspoon salt
> ½ cup milk
> 2 tablespoons margarine or butter, melted
> 1 teaspoon vanilla
> 1 cup sugar
> 2 tablespoons unsweetened cocoa
> Dash salt
> 1⅓ cups water heated to 115 to 120°F.
> Whipped cream or favorite flavor of ice cream

Heat oven to 350°F. Lightly spoon flour into measuring cup; level off. In small bowl, combine flour, ¾ cup sugar, 2 tablespoons cocoa, baking powder and ½ teaspoon salt. Stir in milk, margarine and vanilla until well blended; spread in ungreased 9-inch round or square pan or baking dish.

In small bowl, combine 1 cup sugar, 2 tablespoons cocoa and dash salt; sprinkle evenly over cake batter. Pour **hot** water over sugar mixture. Bake at 350°F. for 35 to 45 minutes or until center is set and firm to the touch. Serve warm with whipped cream or ice cream. 8 servings.

HIGH ALTITUDE—Above 3500 Feet: No change.

NUTRITION INFORMATION PER SERVING

SERVING SIZE: 1/8 OF RECIPE		PERCENT U.S. RDA PER SERVING	
CALORIES	340	PROTEIN	4%
PROTEIN	3g	VITAMIN A	6%
CARBOHYDRATE	63g	VITAMIN C	*
FAT	9g	THIAMINE	8%
CHOLESTEROL	20mg	RIBOFLAVIN	8%
SODIUM	320mg	NIACIN	6%
POTASSIUM	75mg	CALCIUM	6%
		IRON	6%

*Contains less than 2% of the U.S. RDA of this nutrient.

Dinner guests will be impressed by this chocolate and cherry favorite. It can be made early in the day since it refrigerates well.

BLACK FOREST TART

15-oz. pkg. Pillsbury All Ready Pie Crusts
  1 teaspoon flour

FILLING

  6 oz. (6 squares) semi-sweet chocolate, cut into pieces
  2 tablespoons margarine or butter
  ¼ cup powdered sugar
8-oz. pkg. cream cheese, softened
21-oz. can cherry fruit pie filling

TOPPING

  1 cup whipping cream, whipped
  1 oz. (1 square) semi-sweet chocolate, grated

Heat oven to 450°F. Prepare pie crust according to package directions for **unfilled one-crust pie** using 9-inch pie pan or 10-inch tart pan with removable bottom. (Refrigerate remaining crust for later use.) Bake at 450°F. for 9 to 11 minutes or until lightly browned. Cool.

In small saucepan, melt 6 oz. chocolate and margarine over low heat, stirring constantly; remove from heat. In small bowl, beat powdered sugar and cream cheese. Stir in melted chocolate mixture; beat until smooth. Add 1 cup of the cherry pie filling; blend gently. Set aside remaining pie filling. Spread mixture evenly into cooled crust. Refrigerate 1 hour.

In small bowl, combine topping ingredients. Spread evenly over cooled chocolate layer. Spoon remaining cherry pie filling in a band around outer edge of tart. Refrigerate until serving time. Garnish as desired. 8 to 12 servings.

NUTRITION INFORMATION PER SERVING

SERVING SIZE: 1/12 OF RECIPE		PERCENT U.S. RDA PER SERVING	
CALORIES	430	PROTEIN	4%
PROTEIN	3g	VITAMIN A	15%
CARBOHYDRATE	43g	VITAMIN C	2%
FAT	27g	THIAMINE	*
CHOLESTEROL	50mg	RIBOFLAVIN	4%
SODIUM	160mg	NIACIN	*
POTASSIUM	140mg	CALCIUM	4%
		IRON	4%

*Contains less than 2% of the U.S. RDA of this nutrient.

Black Forest Tart, Chocolate Filigree Heart p. 47

COOK'S NOTE
GRATED CHOCOLATE SUCCESS
To prevent chocolate from crumbling into brittle pieces when making **Black Forest Tart** or **Hazelnut Praline Chocolate Heart Cake**, microwave 1 ounce semi-sweet chocolate on DEFROST for 20 to 40 seconds before grating.

A chocolate marshmallow refrigerated pie is perfect for that club meeting at your house. Pipe the whipped cream over the top for an elegant touch.

CHOCOLATE MARSHMALLOW MOUSSE PIE

15-oz. pkg. Pillsbury All Ready Pie Crusts
1 teaspoon flour

FILLING
¼ cup firmly packed brown sugar
3 tablespoons cornstarch
¼ teaspoon salt
1½ cups milk
6 oz. (6 squares) semi-sweet chocolate, chopped
2 teaspoons vanilla
1 cup miniature marshmallows
1 cup whipping cream
¼ cup powdered sugar
½ cup chopped pecans
Whipping cream, whipped, sweetened
8 pecan halves, if desired

Heat oven to 450°F. Prepare pie crust according to package directions for **unfilled one-crust pie** using 9-inch pie pan. (Refrigerate remaining crust for later use.) Bake at 450°F. for 9 to 11 minutes or until lightly browned. Cool.

In medium saucepan, combine brown sugar, cornstarch and salt; mix well. Gradually add milk and cook over medium heat until mixture boils and thickens, stirring constantly with wire whisk. Remove from heat; stir in chocolate and vanilla until mixture is smooth. Cool mixture 5 to 10 minutes. Stir in marshmallows. Refrigerate about 25 minutes or until cool and thickened.

In small bowl, beat 1 cup whipping cream until soft peaks form. Add powdered sugar and beat until stiff peaks form. Fold whipped cream into cooled chocolate mixture. Stir in ½ cup pecans. Pour into cooled pie crust. Refrigerate at least 2 hours or until firm. Garnish with whipped cream and pecan halves or as desired. Store in refrigerator. 8 servings.

NUTRITION INFORMATION PER SERVING

SERVING SIZE: 1/8 OF RECIPE		PERCENT U.S. RDA PER SERVING	
CALORIES	550	PROTEIN	8%
PROTEIN	5g	VITAMIN A	15%
CARBOHYDRATE	48g	VITAMIN C	*
FAT	38g	THIAMINE	2%
CHOLESTEROL	70mg	RIBOFLAVIN	8%
SODIUM	220mg	NIACIN	*
POTASSIUM	240mg	CALCIUM	10%
		IRON	6%

*Contains less than 2% of the U.S. RDA of this nutrient.

This light chocolate-flavored dessert is filled with caramel-coated bananas and chocolate chips. Serve with sweetened whipped cream for the ultimate taste sensation.

CHOCOLATE BANANA PUFFY PANCAKES

PANCAKES

½ cup Pillsbury's BEST® All Purpose or Unbleached Flour
2 tablespoons sugar
2 tablespoons unsweetened cocoa
2 eggs
⅔ cup milk
2 tablespoons margarine or butter

FILLING

2 tablespoons margarine or butter
⅓ cup firmly packed brown sugar
3 medium bananas, diagonally sliced
2 tablespoons miniature semi-sweet chocolate chips
1 cup whipping cream, whipped, sweetened

Heat oven to 425°F. Lightly spoon flour into measuring cup; level off. In small bowl, combine flour, sugar and cocoa; blend well. In medium bowl, beat eggs slightly. Gradually add flour mixture and milk, beating with rotary beater until smooth. Melt 1 tablespoon margarine in each of two 9-inch pie plates in oven; spread to cover bottom. Pour batter into pie plates. Bake at 425°F. for 10 to 15 minutes or until golden brown. (Pancakes will form a well in the center and edges will puff up.)

While pancakes are baking, melt 2 tablespoons margarine in medium skillet. Add brown sugar and bring mixture to a boil over medium heat, stirring constantly. Remove from heat; add bananas. Stir gently until bananas are well coated. Spoon half of filling into each pancake; sprinkle with 1 tablespoon chocolate chips. Cut each pancake into 4 wedges. Top with sweetened whipped cream. Serve immediately. 8 servings.

HIGH ALTITUDE—Above 3500 Feet: No change.

NUTRITION INFORMATION PER SERVING

SERVING SIZE: 1/8 OF RECIPE		PERCENT U.S. RDA PER SERVING	
CALORIES	330	PROTEIN	6%
PROTEIN	4g	VITAMIN A	15%
CARBOHYDRATE	34g	VITAMIN C	4%
FAT	20g	THIAMINE	6%
CHOLESTEROL	110mg	RIBOFLAVIN	10%
SODIUM	120mg	NIACIN	4%
POTASSIUM	310mg	CALCIUM	6%
		IRON	6%

Two delicious brownie layers separated by a raspberry cream filling make a gourmet chocolate dessert. Serve it with a flavored coffee topped with whipped cream.

RASPBERRY CREAM BROWNIE WEDGES

FILLING
8-oz. pkg. cream cheese, softened
½ cup seedless raspberry
    preserves
1 tablespoon flour
1 egg
2 to 3 drops red food coloring*

BROWNIE
¾ cup margarine or butter
4 oz. (4 squares) unsweetened
    chocolate
¾ cup sugar
3 eggs
1 cup Pillsbury's BEST® All
    Purpose or Unbleached
    Flour
½ teaspoon baking powder
¼ teaspoon salt
3 tablespoons raspberry-flavored
    liqueur or water

GLAZE
1 oz. (1 square) white baking bar
2 teaspoons oil

Heat oven to 350°F. Lightly grease 9-inch springform pan. In small bowl, combine all filling ingredients. Beat 1 minute at medium speed; set aside.

In medium saucepan, melt margarine and chocolate over low heat, stirring constantly. Remove from heat; cool slightly. Add sugar and 3 eggs; beat well. Lightly spoon flour into measuring cup; level off. Stir in flour, baking powder and salt; blend well. Stir in raspberry liqueur; blend well. Spread half of chocolate mixture in bottom of greased pan. Spread filling evenly over chocolate. Spread remaining chocolate mixture evenly over filling. Bake at 350°F. for 37 to 42 minutes or until center is set. Cool on wire rack 5 minutes; run knife around edge of pan to loosen. Cool completely; remove from pan.

In small saucepan, melt glaze ingredients over low heat, stirring constantly until smooth. Drizzle glaze over top of brownie; allow to set. Cut into wedges. 12 servings.

TIP: *Use paste food color for more vivid color.

HIGH ALTITUDE—Above 3500 Feet: Decrease sugar to ⅔ cup. Bake as directed above.

NUTRITION INFORMATION PER SERVING

SERVING SIZE:		PERCENT U.S. RDA	
1/12 OF RECIPE		PER SERVING	
CALORIES	410	PROTEIN	8%
PROTEIN	6g	VITAMIN A	15%
CARBOHYDRATE	38g	VITAMIN C	*
FAT	26g	THIAMINE	6%
CHOLESTEROL	110mg	RIBOFLAVIN	10%
SODIUM	280mg	NIACIN	4%
POTASSIUM	160mg	CALCIUM	4%
		IRON	10%

*Contains less than 2% of the U.S. RDA of this nutrient.

COOK'S NOTE
FOOD COLORING IN PASTE FORM

Paste food coloring is most often used by professional cooks or bakers to achieve colors of deep intensity. It comes in small jars and is very thick and easier to control than the liquid variety. A toothpick dipped into paste food coloring and then into icing to be colored offers good color control. Most gourmet houseware shops and cooking catalogs carry it.

Raspberry Cream Brownie Wedge

BROWNIES GALORE

Indulge in these gooey, chewy variations on an American original.

Mystery shrouds the birth of brownies. But whether they were the fortunate result of a failed chocolate cake or conspicuously concocted, there's no deep, dark secret behind their popularity. Just deep, dark chocolate (or white chocolate, or caramel, or mint or peanut butter)!

However, there are a few secrets to baking the best-ever brownies:

- Choose pans specified in the recipe and prepare them according to the directions.
- Mix according to recipe directions being careful not to overmix.
- Bake brownies only for the time indicated in the recipe, or until set. This test for doneness is to feel structure beneath your finger when you lightly press the brownie surface.

Brownies can be as plain as a white-washed farmhouse or as gussied up as a Victorian mansion. With equal aplomb, they adapt to lunchboxes or dessert buffets.

Eight of the brownies presented here are made from a mix. With the fanciful addition of frostings, flavorings, fillings or fruits, they are transformed into gourmet delights. The rest of these confections range from chocolate syrup brownies microwaved in minutes to brownies studded with chunks of white and semi-sweet chocolate.

Pictured clockwise from top: Mint Brownies Supreme p. 29, Irish Coffee Brownies p. 28, Trail Mix Brownies p. 28

Coffee and whiskey flavor these scrumptious brownies. They are topped with a cream cheese frosting.

IRISH COFFEE BROWNIES

BROWNIES

> 1 teaspoon instant coffee
>   granules or crystals
> ¼ cup water
> 21½-oz. pkg. Pillsbury Fudge
>   Brownie Mix
> ½ cup oil
> 1 egg
> ¼ cup whiskey

FROSTING

> ½ teaspoon instant coffee
>   granules or crystals
> 1 tablespoon whiskey
> 2 cups powdered sugar
> 3-oz. pkg. cream cheese, softened
> 3 to 4 teaspoons milk

Heat oven to 350°F. Grease bottom only of 13x9-inch pan. In large bowl, combine 1 teaspoon instant coffee and water; stir until dissolved. Add remaining brownie ingredients; stir 50 strokes with spoon. Spread in greased pan. Bake at 350°F. for 33 to 35 minutes or until set. DO NOT OVERBAKE. Cool completely.

In medium bowl, combine ½ teaspoon instant coffee and 1 tablespoon whiskey; stir until dissolved. Add remaining frosting ingredients, adding enough milk until frosting is of desired spreading consistency; beat until light and fluffy. Spread evenly over cooled bars. Refrigerate until frosting is set. Cut into bars. Store in refrigerator. 36 bars.

HIGH ALTITUDE—Above 3500 Feet: Add ¼ cup flour to dry brownie mix. Bake as directed above.

Trail mix and cinnamon complement the chocolate in this moist and chewy brownie. It's a great brownie to pack in box lunches or to take to an informal social gathering.

TRAIL MIX BROWNIES

> 21½-oz. pkg. Pillsbury Fudge
>   Brownie Mix
> ½ teaspoon cinnamon
> ½ cup water
> ½ cup oil
> 2 eggs
> ½ cup trail mix

Heat oven to 350°F. Grease bottom only of 13x9-inch pan. In large bowl, combine all ingredients except trail mix; beat 50 strokes with spoon. Spread in greased pan. Sprinkle with trail mix. Bake at 350°F. for 33 to 35 minutes or until set. DO NOT OVERBAKE. Cut into bars. 36 bars.

HIGH ALTITUDE—Above 3500 Feet: Add ¼ cup flour to dry brownie mix. Bake as directed above.

NUTRITION INFORMATION PER SERVING

SERVING SIZE: 1 BAR		PERCENT U.S. RDA PER SERVING	
CALORIES	110	PROTEIN	*
PROTEIN	1g	VITAMIN A	*
CARBOHYDRATE	15g	VITAMIN C	*
FAT	5g	THIAMINE	2%
CHOLESTEROL	15mg	RIBOFLAVIN	*
SODIUM	60mg	NIACIN	*
POTASSIUM	55mg	CALCIUM	*
		IRON	2%

*Contains less than 2% of the U.S. RDA of this nutrient.

NUTRITION INFORMATION PER SERVING

SERVING SIZE: 1 BAR		PERCENT U.S. RDA PER SERVING	
CALORIES	130	PROTEIN	*
PROTEIN	1g	VITAMIN A	*
CARBOHYDRATE	20g	VITAMIN C	*
FAT	5g	THIAMINE	2%
CHOLESTEROL	10mg	RIBOFLAVIN	*
SODIUM	65mg	NIACIN	*
POTASSIUM	50mg	CALCIUM	*
		IRON	2%

*Contains less than 2% of the U.S. RDA of this nutrient.

Everyone will rave about these fudge brownies. This recipe makes an ideal dessert for a Mexican or Italian meal.

MINT BROWNIES SUPREME

BROWNIES
21½-oz. pkg. Pillsbury Fudge
      Brownie Mix
  ½ cup water
  ½ cup oil
  1 egg
  ½ teaspoon mint extract

FILLING
  ½ cup margarine or butter,
      softened
3-oz. pkg. cream cheese, softened
2½ cups powdered sugar
  3 tablespoons creme de
      menthe syrup
      Green food coloring, if
      desired

FROSTING
6-oz. pkg. (1 cup) semi-sweet
      chocolate chips
  ⅓ cup margarine

Heat oven to 350°F. Grease bottom only of 13x9-inch pan. In large bowl, combine all brownie ingredients; beat 50 strokes with spoon. Spread in greased pan. Bake at 350°F. for 33 to 35 minutes or until brownies are set. DO NOT OVERBAKE. Cool completely.

In medium bowl, combine ½ cup margarine and cream cheese; beat until light and fluffy. Add powdered sugar, creme de menthe syrup and green food coloring; beat until smooth. Spread evenly over cooled bars.

In small saucepan, melt chocolate and margarine over low heat until smooth, stirring constantly. Remove from heat; cool 15 minutes. Pour frosting evenly over mint filling. Spread carefully to cover filling. Refrigerate 1 hour before cutting. Cut into bars. Garnish as desired. Store in refrigerator. 48 bars.

HIGH ALTITUDE—Above 3500 Feet: Add ¼ cup flour to dry brownie mix. Bake as directed above.

NUTRITION INFORMATION PER SERVING

SERVING SIZE: 1 BAR		PERCENT U.S. RDA PER SERVING	
CALORIES	150	PROTEIN	*
PROTEIN	1g	VITAMIN A	2%
CARBOHYDRATE	18g	VITAMIN C	*
FAT	8g	THIAMINE	*
CHOLESTEROL	8mg	RIBOFLAVIN	*
SODIUM	85mg	NIACIN	*
POTASSIUM	50mg	CALCIUM	*
		IRON	2%

*Contains less than 2% of the U.S. RDA of this nutrient.

BROWNIES GALORE

Have you ever thought of baking brownies into cupcakes? We think you'll love these topped with fluffy maple-flavored frosting.

MAPLE NUT BROWNIE CUPCAKES

BROWNIES
21½-oz. pkg. Pillsbury Fudge
   Brownie Mix
 ½ cup water
 ½ cup oil
 1 teaspoon maple flavoring
 2 eggs
 1 cup coarsely chopped
  walnuts

FROSTING
 ¾ cup Pillsbury Frosting
   Supreme Ready to Spread
   Vanilla Frosting
 ¾ cup whipping cream,
  whipped
 ¼ teaspoon nutmeg
 ¼ teaspoon maple flavoring

Heat oven to 350°F. Line 15 muffin cups with foil liners. In large bowl, combine all brownie ingredients except walnuts; beat 50 strokes with spoon. Spoon about ¼ cup batter into each foil-lined cup; sprinkle each with 1 tablespoon walnuts. Bake at 350°F. for 27 to 32 minutes or until cupcakes are set. DO NOT OVERBAKE. Cool 2 minutes; remove from muffin cups. Cool completely.

In small bowl, combine all frosting ingredients; stir until well blended. Spoon or pipe over cooled brownie cupcakes. 15 cupcakes.

HIGH ALTITUDE—Above 3500 Feet: Add ⅓ cup flour to dry brownie mix. Bake as directed above.

NUTRITION INFORMATION PER SERVING

SERVING SIZE: 1 CUPCAKE		PERCENT U.S. RDA PER SERVING	
CALORIES	380	PROTEIN	6%
PROTEIN	4g	VITAMIN A	4%
CARBOHYDRATE	43g	VITAMIN C	*
FAT	22g	THIAMINE	8%
CHOLESTEROL	50mg	RIBOFLAVIN	6%
SODIUM	170mg	NIACIN	4%
POTASSIUM	160mg	CALCIUM	2%
		IRON	6%

*Contains less than 2% of the U.S. RDA of this nutrient.

Maple Nut Brownie Cupcakes

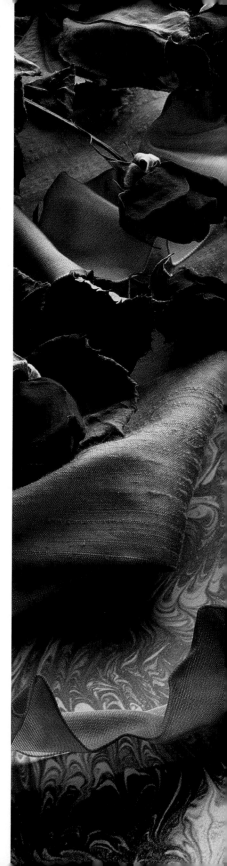

For a tasty combination, a layer of raspberry preserves is included in these scratch brownies. Cut the brownies after they are completely cooled.

RASPBERRY RIBBON BROWNIES

FILLING
8-oz. pkg. cream cheese, softened
⅓ cup sugar
1 egg

BROWNIES
4 oz. (4 squares) unsweetened chocolate, chopped
½ cup margarine or butter
2 cups sugar
1 teaspoon vanilla
4 eggs
1 cup Pillsbury's BEST® All Purpose or Unbleached Flour
½ teaspoon baking powder
½ teaspoon salt
¾ cup raspberry preserves

Heat oven to 350°F. Grease and flour 13x9-inch pan. In small bowl, combine all filling ingredients; blend well. Set aside.

In large saucepan, melt chocolate and margarine over low heat, stirring constantly until smooth. Remove from heat; cool about 15 minutes. Add 2 cups sugar and vanilla; blend well. Beat in 4 eggs, one at a time, blending well after each addition. Lightly spoon flour into measuring cup; level off. Add flour, baking powder and salt to chocolate mixture; stir just until blended. Pour half of chocolate batter into greased and floured pan. Drop filling mixture by teaspoonfuls over chocolate layer; spread carefully to cover chocolate layer. Spoon preserves over filling. Carefully spoon remaining chocolate batter over filling and preserves, spreading to pan edges and smoothing top.

Bake at 350°F. for 45 to 50 minutes or until set. Cool completely. Cut into bars. Store in refrigerator. 48 bars.

HIGH ALTITUDE—Above 3500 Feet: No change.

NUTRITION INFORMATION PER SERVING

SERVING SIZE: 1 BAR		PERCENT U.S. RDA PER SERVING	
CALORIES	120	PROTEIN	2%
PROTEIN	2g	VITAMIN A	2%
CARBOHYDRATE	16g	VITAMIN C	*
FAT	5g	THIAMINE	*
CHOLESTEROL	35mg	RIBOFLAVIN	2%
SODIUM	70mg	NIACIN	*
POTASSIUM	40mg	CALCIUM	*
		IRON	2%

*Contains less than 2% of the U.S. RDA of this nutrient.

COOK'S NOTE

MELTING CHOCOLATE ON THE RANGE TOP

• Chop or grate chocolate for even melting.

• Use a heavy saucepan with flat bottom for even heating.

• Keep utensils dry to prevent moisture from getting into chocolate.

• Use very low heat as chocolate scorches easily.

• Stir chocolate constantly while it melts.

• Remove pan from heat as soon as chocolate is melted.

Two favorite desserts in one—serve as a bar or cut into larger squares and top with ice cream.

PECAN PIE BROWNIES

TOPPING
- ¼ cup margarine or butter
- 2 tablespoons flour
- ¾ cup firmly packed brown sugar
- 2 eggs
- 1 teaspoon vanilla
- 2 cups chopped pecans

BROWNIES
- 21½-oz. pkg. Pillsbury Fudge Brownie Mix
- ½ cup water
- ¼ cup oil
- 1 egg

Heat oven to 350°F. Grease bottom only of 13x9-inch pan. Melt margarine in medium saucepan; stir in flour until smooth. Add brown sugar and 2 eggs; mix well. Cook over medium-low heat for 5 minutes, stirring constantly. Remove from heat; stir in vanilla and pecans. Set aside.

In large bowl, combine all brownie ingredients; beat 50 strokes with spoon. Spread in greased pan. Spoon topping evenly over top. Bake at 350°F. for 30 to 35 minutes or until set. DO NOT OVERBAKE. Cool completely. Cut into bars. 24 bars.

HIGH ALTITUDE—Above 3500 Feet: Add ¼ cup flour to dry brownie mix. Bake as directed above.

NUTRITION INFORMATION PER SERVING

SERVING SIZE: 1 BAR		PERCENT U.S. RDA PER SERVING	
CALORIES	250	PROTEIN	4%
PROTEIN	3g	VITAMIN A	2%
CARBOHYDRATE	30g	VITAMIN C	*
FAT	13g	THIAMINE	6%
CHOLESTEROL	35mg	RIBOFLAVIN	4%
SODIUM	120mg	NIACIN	2%
POTASSIUM	135mg	CALCIUM	*
		IRON	6%

*Contains less than 2% of the U.S. RDA of this nutrient.

A peanut butter-vanilla pudding mixture is the topping for these brownie creations. Serve as bars or cut into squares for dessert.

PEANUT BUTTER BROWNIE SQUARES

BROWNIES
- 21½-oz. pkg. Pillsbury Fudge Brownie Mix
- ½ cup water
- ½ cup oil
- 1 egg
- ½ cup raisins

PUDDING
- 3½-oz. pkg. vanilla flavor instant pudding and pie filling mix
- 1 cup milk
- 1 cup dairy sour cream
- ¼ cup creamy peanut butter
- Raisins or grated chocolate

Heat oven to 350°F. Grease bottom only of 13x9-inch pan. In large bowl, combine all brownie ingredients except raisins; beat 50 strokes with spoon. Stir in ½ cup raisins. Spread in greased pan. Bake at 350°F. for 33 to 35 minutes. DO NOT OVERBAKE. Cool.

In medium bowl, combine all pudding ingredients except raisins; beat 1 minute or until thickened and smooth. Spread over cooled brownies. Garnish with raisins or grated chocolate. Cut into bars or squares. Store in refrigerator. 36 bars or 16 squares.

HIGH ALTITUDE—Above 3500 Feet: Add ¼ cup flour to dry brownie mix. Bake as directed above.

NUTRITION INFORMATION PER SERVING

SERVING SIZE: 1 BAR		PERCENT U.S. RDA PER SERVING	
CALORIES	150	PROTEIN	2%
PROTEIN	2g	VITAMIN A	*
CARBOHYDRATE	20g	VITAMIN C	*
FAT	7g	THIAMINE	2%
CHOLESTEROL	10mg	RIBOFLAVIN	2%
SODIUM	85mg	NIACIN	2%
POTASSIUM	100mg	CALCIUM	2%
		IRON	2%

*Contains less than 2% of the U.S. RDA of this nutrient.

When unexpected company arrives, these microwave brownies can be made quickly from scratch. Top them with vanilla ice cream for a delicious taste treat.

CHOCOLATE SYRUP MICROWAVE BROWNIES

BROWNIES
- ½ cup margarine or butter, softened
- ½ cup sugar
- 2 eggs
- ½ cup chocolate-flavored syrup
- 2 teaspoons vanilla
- ¾ cup Pillsbury's BEST® All Purpose or Unbleached Flour
- ¼ teaspoon salt

FROSTING
- 1 cup powdered sugar
- 2 tablespoons chocolate-flavored syrup
- 1 tablespoon margarine or butter, softened
- 2 to 4 teaspoons milk

▦ MICROWAVE DIRECTIONS: Grease 10x6-inch (1½-quart) microwave-safe dish. In medium bowl, combine ½ cup margarine and sugar; beat until light and fluffy. Add eggs, ½ cup chocolate-flavored syrup and vanilla; beat well. Lightly spoon flour into measuring cup; level off. Stir in flour and salt. Pour into greased dish. Microwave on MEDIUM for 8 minutes, rotating dish ½ turn halfway through cooking. Microwave on HIGH for 2 to 3 minutes or until center is set. Cool completely on flat surface.

In small bowl, combine all frosting ingredients, adding enough milk until frosting is of desired spreading consistency; beat until smooth. Spread over cooled brownies. Cut into bars. 12 to 16 servings.

HIGH ALTITUDE—Above 3500 Feet: Increase flour to 1 cup. Bake in greased 9-inch round microwave-safe pan. Microwave on MEDIUM for 8 minutes, rotating dish every 2 minutes. Microwave on HIGH for 1 to 2 minutes or until center is set.

NUTRITION INFORMATION PER SERVING

SERVING SIZE: 1/16 OF RECIPE		PERCENT U.S. RDA PER SERVING	
CALORIES	170	PROTEIN	2%
PROTEIN	2g	VITAMIN A	6%
CARBOHYDRATE	24g	VITAMIN C	*
FAT	7g	THIAMINE	2%
CHOLESTEROL	35mg	RIBOFLAVIN	2%
SODIUM	130mg	NIACIN	*
POTASSIUM	45mg	CALCIUM	*
		IRON	2%

*Contains less than 2% of the U.S. RDA of this nutrient.

Chocolate Syrup Microwave Brownies

Make these irresistible brownies and frost them with rich gooey chocolate.

CHOCOLATE FROSTED TOFFEES

BROWNIES
- ¾ cup Pillsbury's BEST® All Purpose or Unbleached Flour
- ⅓ cup firmly packed brown sugar
- ¼ teaspoon salt
- ¼ cup margarine or butter, softened
- 14-oz. can sweetened condensed milk (not evaporated)
- ½ cup dark corn syrup
- 2 teaspoons vanilla
- 4 cups flaked coconut, toasted*

FROSTING
- 6-oz. pkg. (1 cup) semi-sweet chocolate chips
- 3 to 4 tablespoons whipping cream or milk
- ½ cup powdered sugar
- 2 tablespoons margarine or butter, softened
- 1 teaspoon vanilla

Heat oven to 350°F. Generously grease 13x9-inch pan. Lightly spoon flour into measuring cup; level off. In large bowl, combine all brownie ingredients except coconut; mix well. Stir in coconut. Spread in greased pan. Bake at 350°F. for 25 to 35 minutes or until golden brown. Cool.

In small saucepan, heat chocolate chips in whipping cream over low heat, stirring constantly. Stir in powdered sugar, 2 tablespoons margarine and 1 teaspoon vanilla; mix well. Spread over cooled bars. Refrigerate 30 minutes; cut into bars. 48 bars.

TIP: *To toast coconut, spread on cookie sheet, bake at 350°F. for 12 to 16 minutes or until golden brown.

HIGH ALTITUDE—Above 3500 Feet: No change.

NUTRITION INFORMATION PER SERVING

SERVING SIZE: 1 BAR		PERCENT U.S. RDA PER SERVING	
CALORIES	130	PROTEIN	2%
PROTEIN	1g	VITAMIN A	2%
CARBOHYDRATE	17g	VITAMIN C	*
FAT	6g	THIAMINE	*
CHOLESTEROL	4mg	RIBOFLAVIN	2%
SODIUM	45mg	NIACIN	*
POTASSIUM	85mg	CALCIUM	4%
		IRON	2%

*Contains less than 2% of the U.S. RDA of this nutrient.

The brownies taste like a gourmet delight but take little time to prepare. Cut into attractive bars using a hot, wet knife.

FROSTED ORANGE CAPPUCCINO BROWNIES

BROWNIES

1 to 2 tablespoons instant coffee
  granules or crystals
½ cup water
21½-oz. pkg. Pillsbury Fudge
  Brownie Mix
½ cup oil
1 tablespoon brandy*
1 tablespoon grated orange
  peel
1 egg

FROSTING

1 can Pillsbury Frosting
  Supreme Ready to Spread
  Chocolate Fudge Frosting

GLAZE

¼ cup powdered sugar
½ teaspoon grated orange peel
1 to 2 teaspoons water

Heat oven to 350°F. Grease bottom only of 13x9-inch pan. In large bowl, dissolve instant coffee in water. Add remaining brownie ingredients; beat 50 strokes with spoon. Spread in greased pan. Bake at 350°F. for 30 to 35 minutes or until set. DO NOT OVERBAKE. Cool completely.

Frost cooled brownies with frosting. In small bowl, combine all glaze ingredients, adding enough water for desired glaze consistency. Drizzle over frosting; allow to set. Cut into bars. 36 bars.

TIP: *One teaspoon brandy extract plus 2 teaspoons water can be substituted for brandy.

HIGH ALTITUDE—Above 3500 Feet: Add ¼ cup flour to dry brownie mix. Bake as directed above.

NUTRITION INFORMATION PER SERVING
SERVING SIZE: PERCENT U.S. RDA
1 BAR   PER SERVING
CALORIES   150   PROTEIN   *
PROTEIN   1g   VITAMIN A   *
CARBOHYDRATE 23g   VITAMIN C   *
FAT   6g   THIAMINE   2%
CHOLESTEROL   8mg   RIBOFLAVIN   *
SODIUM   85mg   NIACIN   2%
POTASSIUM   85mg   CALCIUM   *
                     IRON   2%
*Contains less than 2% of the U.S. RDA of this nutrient.

This is a chewy chocolate brownie filled with raisins and topped with walnuts. The semi-sweet chocolate glaze offers an outstanding fudgy taste.

GLAZED RAISIN BROWNIES

BROWNIES
21½-oz. pkg. Pillsbury Fudge
  Brownie Mix
½ cup water
½ cup oil
1 egg
⅔ cup raisins
½ cup chopped walnuts

GLAZE
½ cup semi-sweet chocolate
  chips
2 tablespoons margarine

Heat oven to 350°F. Grease bottom only of 13x9-inch pan. In large bowl, combine brownie mix, water, oil and egg; beat 50 strokes with spoon. Stir in raisins. Spread in greased pan; sprinkle with walnuts. Bake at 350°F. for 33 to 35 minutes or until set. DO NOT OVERBAKE. Cool completely.

In small saucepan, melt chocolate chips and margarine over low heat, stirring constantly. Drizzle evenly over cooled bars. Refrigerate 1 hour or until glaze is set. Cut into bars. 36 bars.

HIGH ALTITUDE—Above 3500 Feet: Add ¼ cup flour to dry brownie mix. Bake as directed above.

NUTRITION INFORMATION PER SERVING
SERVING SIZE: PERCENT U.S. RDA
1 BAR   PER SERVING
CALORIES   140   PROTEIN   2%
PROTEIN   1g   VITAMIN A   *
CARBOHYDRATE 18g   VITAMIN C   *
FAT   7g   THIAMINE   2%
CHOLESTEROL   8mg   RIBOFLAVIN   2%
SODIUM   65mg   NIACIN   *
POTASSIUM   80mg   CALCIUM   *
                     IRON   2%
*Contains less than 2% of the U.S. RDA of this nutrient.

Loaded with chunks of semi-sweet chocolate, one wedge of these blonde brownies won't be enough! Cover the pan tightly with foil to maintain freshness.

WHITE CHOCOLATE CHUNK BROWNIE WEDGES

BROWNIES
- ½ cup margarine or butter
- 4 oz. (4 squares) white baking bar, cut into pieces
- 2 eggs
- ⅛ teaspoon salt
- ½ cup sugar
- 1½ teaspoons vanilla
- 1¼ cups Pillsbury's BEST® All Purpose or Unbleached Flour
- 2 oz. (2 squares) semi-sweet chocolate, cut into pieces

GLAZE
- 1 oz. (1 square) semi-sweet chocolate
- 2 teaspoons margarine

Heat oven to 350°F. Grease and flour 9-inch round cake pan. In small saucepan, melt ½ cup margarine and 2 oz. of the white baking bar over low heat, stirring constantly until melted. Remove from heat; set aside.

In small bowl, combine eggs and salt; beat until frothy. Add sugar and continue beating for about 3 minutes or until light in color and thickened. Add melted chocolate mixture and vanilla; blend well. Lightly spoon flour into measuring cup; level off. Stir in flour; mix well. Fold in remaining white chocolate pieces and semi-sweet chocolate pieces. Spread in greased and floured pan. Bake at 350°F. for 23 to 28 minutes or until toothpick inserted in center comes out clean. Cool on wire rack.

In small saucepan, melt glaze ingredients until smooth, stirring constantly. Spoon over cooled brownies. Allow to set. Cut into wedges. 12 servings.

HIGH ALTITUDE—Above 3500 Feet: Increase flour to 1⅓ cups. Bake as directed above.

NUTRITION INFORMATION PER SERVING

SERVING SIZE: 1/12 OF RECIPE		PERCENT U.S. RDA PER SERVING	
CALORIES	260	PROTEIN	4%
PROTEIN	3g	VITAMIN A	8%
CARBOHYDRATE	28g	VITAMIN C	*
FAT	15g	THIAMINE	6%
CHOLESTEROL	50mg	RIBOFLAVIN	6%
SODIUM	140mg	NIACIN	4%
POTASSIUM	80mg	CALCIUM	2%
		IRON	4%

*Contains less than 2% of the U.S. RDA of this nutrient.

White Chocolate Chunk Brownie Wedges,
Chocolate-Dipped Strawberries p. 41

Caramel flavor dominates this bar full of crunchy cashews. These brownies bake in an 8 or 9-inch pan, just the perfect size to take to a small family gathering.

FROSTED BLONDE CASHEW BROWNIES

BROWNIES

    1 cup salted cashews
    1 cup firmly packed brown sugar
    ⅓ cup oil
    1 teaspoon vanilla
    2 eggs
    1¼ cups Pillsbury's BEST® All
           Purpose or Unbleached Flour
    1 teaspoon baking powder
    ¼ teaspoon salt, if desired

FROSTING

    3 oz. (3 squares) white baking bar,
           cut into pieces
    2 tablespoons margarine or butter,
           softened
    2 tablespoons milk
    1 cup powdered sugar

Heat oven to 350°F. Grease 8 or 9-inch square pan. In food processor bowl with metal blade or blender container, process ½ cup of the cashews until mixture resembles coarse crumbs; place in medium bowl. Coarsely chop remaining cashews; set aside. Add brown sugar, oil, vanilla and eggs to ground cashews; beat well. Lightly spoon flour into measuring cup; level off. Add flour, baking powder, salt and chopped cashews; mix well. Spread in greased pan. Bake at 350°F. for 20 to 30 minutes or until toothpick inserted in center comes out clean. Cool completely.

Melt white baking bar in small saucepan over low heat, stirring constantly; remove from heat. Beat in margarine, milk and powdered sugar until mixture is smooth. Spread evenly over cooled bars. Cut into bars. 25 bars

HIGH ALTITUDE—Above 3500 Feet: Decrease brown sugar to ¾ cup; increase flour to 1½ cups. Bake as directed above.

NUTRITION INFORMATION PER SERVING

SERVING SIZE: 1 BAR		PERCENT U.S. RDA PER SERVING	
CALORIES	160	PROTEIN	2%
PROTEIN	2g	VITAMIN A	*
CARBOHYDRATE	21g	VITAMIN C	*
FAT	8g	THIAMINE	4%
CHOLESTEROL	25mg	RIBOFLAVIN	2%
SODIUM	55mg	NIACIN	2%
POTASSIUM	85mg	CALCIUM	2%
		IRON	6%

*Contains less than 2% of the U.S. RDA of this nutrient.

COOK'S NOTE

WHITE CHOCOLATE UPDATE

White chocolate, popular in recipes today, is not really chocolate at all but a combination of cocoa butter, sugar, milk and flavorings. It is available in several forms in most supermarkets.

Please note which variety of white chocolate appears in each recipe ingredient list, as the correct form of white chocolate is critical for optimum performance.

- **White baking bar** is a high quality bar form of white chocolate. It contains the greatest amount of cocoa butter and is called for in many Pillsbury recipes.

- **Vanilla-flavored candy coating** is most commonly known as white almond bark. It contains higher amounts of sugar and less cocoa butter than the white baking bar.

- **Vanilla milk chips** are similar in quality to white baking bar. They are available in a regular-sized chip and a large disk-like form. Vanilla milk chips melt well for use in glazes and fillings.

Your family and friends will love these brownies topped with peanuts, marshmallow and milk chocolate.

TIN ROOF SUNDAE BARS

BASE

    21½-oz. pkg. Pillsbury Fudge
            Brownie Mix
      ½ cup water
      ½ cup oil
      1 egg

TOPPING

      7-oz. jar marshmallow creme
     1½ cups peanuts
5 (1.65-oz.) milk chocolate candy
            bars, broken into
            sections

Heat oven to 350°F. Grease bottom only of 13x9-inch pan. In large bowl, combine brownie mix, water, oil and egg; beat 50 strokes with spoon. Spread in greased pan. Bake at 350°F. for 33 to 35 minutes. DO NOT OVERBAKE. Remove from oven; immediately spread marshmallow creme over baked base. Sprinkle evenly with peanuts; top with candy bar sections. Return to oven for 2 minutes or until chocolate is melted. Spread evenly to cover. Cool completely. Cut into bars. 36 bars.

HIGH ALTITUDE—Above 3500 Feet: Add ¼ cup flour to dry brownie mix. Bake as directed above.

NUTRITION INFORMATION PER SERVING

SERVING SIZE: 1 BAR		PERCENT U.S. RDA PER SERVING	
CALORIES	190	PROTEIN	4%
PROTEIN	3g	VITAMIN A	*
CARBOHYDRATE	24g	VITAMIN C	*
FAT	10g	THIAMINE	4%
CHOLESTEROL	9mg	RIBOFLAVIN	2%
SODIUM	120mg	NIACIN	6%
POTASSIUM	115mg	CALCIUM	2%
		IRON	2%

*Contains less than 2% of the U.S. RDA of this nutrient.

These delectable strawberries are perfect as a garnish for a chocolate dessert or served alone as a light dessert.

CHOCOLATE-DIPPED STRAWBERRIES

  36 large strawberries

DARK CHOCOLATE COATING

  ½ cup semi-sweet chocolate chips
  1 teaspoon oil

WHITE CHOCOLATE COATING

  ½ cup vanilla milk chips*
 1½ teaspoons oil

Wash strawberries; gently pat dry. Line tray with waxed paper. In small saucepan over low heat, melt chocolate chips and 1 teaspoon oil, stirring occasionally until smooth. Remove from heat. Set saucepan in pan of hot water to maintain dipping consistency. Dip each strawberry into chocolate mixture until ⅔ of strawberry is coated. Allow excess chocolate to drip off; place strawberries stem side down on prepared tray. Refrigerate until serving time. Repeat using vanilla milk chips and 1½ teaspoons oil. 36 berries.

MICROWAVE DIRECTIONS: In small microwave-safe bowl, combine chocolate chips and 1 teaspoon oil. Microwave on MEDIUM for 1½ to 2½ minutes or until chips are softened; stir until smooth. Continue as directed above. Repeat using vanilla milk chips and 1½ teaspoons oil.

TIP: *To make pastel colored coating, add 3 to 5 drops food coloring to melted vanilla milk chip mixture.

NUTRITION INFORMATION PER SERVING

SERVING SIZE: 1 STRAWBERRY		PERCENT U.S. RDA PER SERVING	
CALORIES	35	PROTEIN	*
PROTEIN	0g	VITAMIN A	*
CARBOHYDRATE	4g	VITAMIN C	15%
FAT	2g	THIAMINE	*
CHOLESTEROL	0mg	RIBOFLAVIN	*
SODIUM	0mg	NIACIN	*
POTASSIUM	45mg	CALCIUM	*
		IRON	*

*Contains less than 2% of the U.S. RDA of this nutrient.

SWEETHEART SPECIALS

Speak the language of love with a gift of chocolate from the heart.

❤

Oh, how I love you! Let me count the ways: *Chocolate Cherry Cordial Cookies* (I love you.) *Glazed Brownie Hearts* (I love you.) *Hazelnut Praline Chocolate Heart Cake* (I love you.)

This collection of heavenly heart-felt confections lets you say "I love you" fifteen different ways. For birthdays, anniversaries and Valentine's Day. For special and not-so-special occasions. For dessert, for brunch, for stolen moments in a busy day.

When creating these sweets for your sweet, create an atmosphere, too. Wrap *Chocolate Shortbread Hearts* in colored cellophane and tie with colorful ribbons. Serve *Chocolate Orange Cheesecake* on a heart-shaped plate or lacy doilies. Tuck *Chocolate Meringue Kisses* into a heart-shaped tin. Present *Chocolate Waffles with Strawberries* for brunch amidst a spray of flowers. Tie a filigreed photograph frame onto a beribboned box of *Pat-in-Pan Fudge*. Homemade chocolate specials send a message of love.

Hazelnut Praline Chocolate Heart Cake p. 44

This is a delicious chocolate cake to serve for a special birthday or Valentine's Day party. A yummy praline layer makes it unusually moist.

HAZELNUT PRALINE CHOCOLATE HEART CAKE

CAKE

- ½ cup butter or margarine
- ¼ cup whipping cream
- 1 cup firmly packed brown sugar
- ¾ cup coarsely chopped hazelnuts
- 1 pkg. Pillsbury Plus Devil's Food Cake Mix
- 1¼ cups water
- ⅓ cup oil
- 3 eggs

TOPPING

- 1¾ cups whipping cream
- ¼ cup powdered sugar
- 1 oz. (1 square) semi-sweet chocolate, grated

Heat oven to 325°F. In small heavy saucepan, combine butter, ¼ cup whipping cream and brown sugar; cook over low heat until butter is melted, stirring constantly. Pour evenly into one 9-inch round and one 9-inch square pan; sprinkle evenly with hazelnuts.* In large bowl, combine cake mix, water, oil and eggs at low speed until moistened; beat 2 minutes at highest speed. Carefully spoon about ¼ of batter over hazelnut mixture around edges of each pan; spoon remaining batter into center of pans.

Bake at 325°F. for 35 to 45 minutes or until cake springs back when touched lightly in center. Cool 5 minutes; remove from pans. Cool completely.

In small bowl, beat 1¾ cups whipping cream until soft peaks form. Blend in powdered sugar and chocolate. To assemble cake, cover 18x14-inch heavy cardboard with foil or colored paper. Cut 9-inch round cake in half vertical. Following diagram, arrange square cake and round cake halves on foil-covered cardboard to form heart. Pipe or spoon topping in decorative design over top of cake. Garnish as desired. Store in refrigerator. 12 to 16 servings.

TIP: *One 8-inch square and one 8-inch round cake pan can be substituted. Bake at 325°F. 42 to 48 minutes.

HIGH ALTITUDE—Above 3500 Feet: Add ¼ c flour to dry cake mix. Increase water to 1⅓ cup. Bake as directed above.

NUTRITION INFORMATION PER SERVING

SERVING SIZE: 1/16 OF RECIPE		PERCENT U.S. RDA PER SERVING	
CALORIES	440	PROTEIN	6%
PROTEIN	4g	VITAMIN A	15%
CARBOHYDRATE	42g	VITAMIN C	*
FAT	29g	THIAMINE	6%
CHOLESTEROL	110mg	RIBOFLAVIN	6%
SODIUM	330mg	NIACIN	2%
POTASSIUM	240mg	CALCIUM	10%
		IRON	8%

*Contains less than 2% of the U.S. RDA of this nutrient.

Hazelnut Praline Chocolate Heart Cake Diagram

Show how much you care by making this luscious cake for your Valentine.

CHOCOLATE LOVERS' CAKE

CAKE
- 1 pkg. Pillsbury Plus Devil's Food Cake Mix
- 1 cup dairy sour cream
- ¾ cup water
- ⅓ cup oil
- 3 eggs
- 4-oz. bar milk chocolate, grated

FILLING
- 1 cup whipping cream, whipped, sweetened
- 21-oz. can cherry fruit pie filling
- ¼ cup sliced almonds
- Chocolate Curls, if desired (this page)

Heat oven to 350°F. Grease and flour two 9-inch round cake pans. In large bowl, combine all cake ingredients except grated chocolate; beat at low speed until moistened; beat 2 minutes at highest speed. Gently fold in grated chocolate. Pour batter evenly into greased and floured pans. Bake at 350°F. for 35 to 45 minutes or until cake springs back when touched lightly in center. Cool 15 minutes; remove from pans. Cool completely.

Place 1 cake layer, bottom side up, on serving plate. Spoon or pipe 1 cup of the whipped cream around top edge of cake. Spoon half of cherry filling over center of cake. Top with remaining cake layer, bottom side down. Spoon remaining cherry filling in heart shape over center of cake. Spoon or pipe remaining whipped cream around edge of heart. Garnish with almonds and Chocolate Curls. Store in refrigerator. 16 servings.

HIGH ALTITUDE—Above 3500 Feet: Add ¼ cup flour to dry cake mix. Increase water to 1⅓ cups. Bake at 375°F. for 30 to 40 minutes.

COOK'S NOTE
CHOCOLATE CURL KNOW-HOW

Giant Chocolate Curls
Cut twelve 4½-inch squares of heavy aluminum foil. Melt 4 oz. (4 squares) semi-sweet chocolate with 2 teaspoons shortening. Using back of teaspoon, spread a layer of chocolate over foil to within 1 inch of each edge. Refrigerate 3 to 4 minutes or until chocolate is just set but not hard and brittle. If desired, sprinkle lightly with powdered sugar. Bring 2 edges of foil together to form a cone shape, crimping edges together. (Do not overlap chocolate.) Refrigerate about 30 minutes or until firm. Working with one at a time, carefully remove foil; keep remaining curls refrigerated. Use to garnish dessert.

Large Chocolate Curls
Melt 4 oz. (4 squares) semi-sweet chocolate. With spatula, spread melted chocolate in thin layers on inverted cookie sheets. Refrigerate until just firm but not brittle, about 10 minutes. Using metal spatula or pancake turner, scrape chocolate from pan making curls. The width of the spatula will determine the width of the curls. Transfer curls to dessert using a toothpick.

Small Chocolate Curls
Place one or more squares of semi-sweet chocolate on a piece of foil. Let stand in warm place (80 to 85°F.) for 5 to 10 minutes or until slightly softened. With a vegetable peeler and using long strokes, shave chocolate from the bottom of the square. Milk chocolate curls can be made using a thick milk chocolate bar and this method.

These seasonally festive puffs shaped into hearts make the perfect dessert for your special person. The cream and caramel filling is very easy and not too sweet.

CHOCOLATE CREAM PUFF HEARTS

PUFFS

    1 cup Pillsbury's BEST® All Purpose or Unbleached Flour

    1 cup water

    ½ cup margarine or butter

    1 oz. (1 square) semi-sweet chocolate

    ¼ teaspoon salt

    4 eggs

FILLING

    2 cups whipping cream

2 to 3 tablespoons powdered sugar

    1 cup caramel ice cream topping

    ¼ cup chopped pecans

Heat oven to 375°F. Grease cookie sheets. Lightly spoon flour into measuring cup; level off. In medium saucepan, combine water, margarine, chocolate and salt over medium heat until mixture comes to a boil. Reduce heat to low. Add flour, beating vigorously until mixture leaves sides o pan; remove from heat. Place mixture in large mixing bowl. Add eggs, one at a time, beating with electric mixer at medium speed for 1 minute after each addition; beat until smooth and glossy. DO NOT OVERBEAT. To form each puff, spoon about ¼ cup dough onto greased cookie sheet. Using table knife form heart shape by placing knife at edge of dough and pulling inward ½ inch. Using knife, shape bottom of puff into point.

Bake at 375°F. for 40 to 45 minutes or until puffed and browned. With sharp knife, pierce side of each puff to allow steam to escape. Remove from cookie sheets; cool on wire rack.

In large bowl, beat whipping cream at highest speed until soft peaks form; add powdered sugar, beating until stiff peaks form. Fold in ⅓ cup of the caramel ice cream topping and pecans

To serve, split puffs; remove filaments of soft dough. Fill each puff with abou ⅓ cup filling. Drizzle remaining caramel ice cream topping over tops o puffs. 12 puffs.

HIGH ALTITUDE—Above 3500 Feet: No chang

NUTRITION INFORMATION PER SERVING

SERVING SIZE: 1 PUFF		PERCENT U.S. RDA PER SERVING	
CALORIES	390	PROTEIN	8%
PROTEIN	6g	VITAMIN A	20%
CARBOHYDRATE	31g	VITAMIN C	*
FAT	27g	THIAMINE	6%
CHOLESTEROL	150mg	RIBOFLAVIN	8%
SODIUM	230mg	NIACIN	2%
POTASSIUM	80mg	CALCIUM	4%
		IRON	4%

*Contains less than 2% of the U.S. RDA of this nutrient.

This is an absolutely spectacular dessert for a special occasion!

FROZEN RASPBERRY MACADAMIA DESSERT

CRUST

- 1 cup (20 wafers) crushed vanilla wafers
- ½ cup finely chopped macadamia nuts or almonds
- ¼ cup margarine or butter, melted

FILLING

- 14-oz. can sweetened condensed milk (not evaporated)
- 3 tablespoons lemon juice
- 3 tablespoons orange-flavored liqueur or orange juice
- 10-oz. pkg. frozen raspberries with syrup, thawed
- 1 cup whipping cream, whipped Chocolate Filigree Hearts (this page)

Heat oven to 375°F. In small bowl, combine all crust ingredients; mix well. Press firmly in bottom of 8-inch springform pan. Bake at 375°F. for 8 to 10 minutes. Cool.

In large bowl, combine sweetened condensed milk, lemon juice and liqueur; beat until smooth. Add raspberries; beat at low speed until well blended. Fold in whipped cream. Pour over cooled crust. Freeze until firm. Just before serving, let stand at room temperature about 15 minutes. Garnish with Chocolate Filigree Hearts. 12 servings.

NUTRITION INFORMATION PER SERVING

SERVING SIZE: 1/12 OF RECIPE		PERCENT U.S. RDA PER SERVING	
CALORIES	390	PROTEIN	8%
PROTEIN	5g	VITAMIN A	10%
CARBOHYDRATE	44g	VITAMIN C	10%
FAT	22g	THIAMINE	6%
CHOLESTEROL	45mg	RIBOFLAVIN	15%
SODIUM	130mg	NIACIN	2%
POTASSIUM	250mg	CALCIUM	15%
		IRON	4%

Make these unique chocolate heart garnishes to top off Frozen Raspberry Macadamia Dessert.

CHOCOLATE FILIGREE HEARTS

- 2 oz. (2 squares) semi-sweet chocolate
- 2 teaspoons shortening

Draw 1 pattern of heart design on white paper. Cut twelve 3x3-inch squares of waxed paper. Set aside.

In small saucepan, melt chocolate with shortening over low heat, stirring constantly. Cool slightly. Pour chocolate mixture into small squeeze bottle or pastry bag with small writing tip. Place pattern piece on cookie sheet. Lay waxed paper square over pattern. Pipe chocolate over outline. (Chocolate lines should be about ¼ inch wide.) Carefully slip out pattern piece. Repeat, making 12 filigree hearts. Refrigerate 30 minutes or until ready to use. Carefully peel off waxed paper; place on dessert. 12 filigree hearts.

NUTRITION INFORMATION PER SERVING

SERVING SIZE: 1 HEART		PERCENT U.S. RDA PER SERVING	
CALORIES	30	PROTEIN	*
PROTEIN	0g	VITAMIN A	*
CARBOHYDRATE	3g	VITAMIN C	*
FAT	2g	THIAMINE	*
CHOLESTEROL	0mg	RIBOFLAVIN	*
SODIUM	0mg	NIACIN	*
POTASSIUM	15mg	CALCIUM	*
		IRON	*

*Contains less than 2% of the U.S. RDA of this nutrient.

Serve for a special-day breakfast or as a shortcake-like dessert. Using a heart-shaped waffle iron will make this recipe fit the occasion.

CHOCOLATE WAFFLES WITH STRAWBERRIES

   1 cup Hungry Jack® Buttermilk Pancake and Waffle Mix
   ¼ cup unsweetened cocoa
   ⅔ cup milk
   2 tablespoons oil
   1 egg
      Whipped cream, sweetened
10-oz. pkg. frozen strawberries with syrup, thawed

Heat waffle iron. In medium bowl, combine pancake mix and cocoa; blend well. Add milk, oil and egg; stir until all dry particles are moistened. Bake in hot waffle iron until steaming stops. Top with whipped cream; spoon strawberries over whipped cream. 6 waffles.

TIP: Thawed strawberries with syrup can be pureed in blender or food processor to make syrup. If desired, fresh strawberries can be used as garnish.

NUTRITION INFORMATION PER SERVING

SERVING SIZE: 1 WAFFLE		PERCENT U.S. RDA PER SERVING	
CALORIES	310	PROTEIN	8%
PROTEIN	5g	VITAMIN A	8%
CARBOHYDRATE	38g	VITAMIN C	70%
FAT	15g	THIAMINE	10%
CHOLESTEROL	80mg	RIBOFLAVIN	10%
SODIUM	400mg	NIACIN	6%
POTASSIUM	200mg	CALCIUM	8%
		IRON	8%

Chocolate Waffles With Strawberries

49

Heat oven to 350°F. Grease 15x10x1-inch baking pan. In large bowl, combine almond paste and margarine; blend until smooth. Add sugar, brown sugar, eggs, almond extract and salt; mix well. Lightly spoon flour into measuring cup; level off. Add flour gradually, stirring to form a smooth dough. Divide dough in half.

To prepare decorative top crust, roll half of dough between 2 sheets of waxed paper to form 15x10-inch rectangle. Remove top sheet of waxed paper. Using small heart-shaped canape cutter, in 6 rows of 8 hearts each, cut out 48 hearts. Set decorative crust aside. Add cutout pieces to remaining half of dough.

With floured fingers, press remaining dough in bottom of greased pan. Bake at 350°F. for 10 minutes; cool 5 minutes. Spread evenly with raspberry preserves; sprinkle with almonds and chocolate chips. Lifting decorative top crust by waxed paper, place crust, dough side down, over filling; carefully remove waxed paper. Trim edges if necessary. Bake at 350°F. for 20 to 25 minutes or until golden brown. Cool completely. Dust with powdered sugar. Cut into 48 bars with heart cutout centered on each. Store in tightly covered container. 4 dozen bars

HIGH ALTITUDE—Above 3500 Feet: No change

This recipe is a version of a European pastry, so plan to take some extra time when preparing it. Use any canape cutter design you wish to make the cutouts.

CHOCOLATE ALMOND LINZER BARS

3.5-oz. pkg. almond paste, softened
½ cup margarine or butter, softened
½ cup sugar
½ cup firmly packed brown sugar
2 eggs
1 teaspoon almond extract
¼ teaspoon salt
3 cups Pillsbury's BEST® All Purpose or Unbleached Flour
1½ cups raspberry preserves
½ cup sliced almonds
½ cup miniature semi-sweet chocolate chips
Powdered sugar

NUTRITION INFORMATION PER SERVING

SERVING SIZE: 1 BAR		PERCENT U.S. RDA PER SERVING	
CALORIES	120	PROTEIN	2%
PROTEIN	2g	VITAMIN A	*
CARBOHYDRATE	19g	VITAMIN C	*
FAT	4g	THIAMINE	4%
CHOLESTEROL	10mg	RIBOFLAVIN	4%
SODIUM	40mg	NIACIN	2%
POTASSIUM	55mg	CALCIUM	*
		IRON	4%

*Contains less than 2% of the U.S. RDA of this nutrient.

A heart-shaped dessert layered with lemon cream filling and strawberries and glazed with chocolate makes the perfect Valentine's Day surprise.

SWEETHEART LEMON CREAM TORTE

15-oz. pkg. Pillsbury All Ready Pie
    Crusts
  2 teaspoons flour

FILLING
  ⅓ cup sugar
  3 tablespoons cornstarch
  ¼ teaspoon salt
1⅓ cups milk
  ¼ cup lemon juice
  2 egg yolks
  1 tablespoon margarine or
    butter
  1 cup whipping cream
  2 tablespoons powdered sugar

TOPPING
 12 large strawberries, halved
  2 tablespoons semi-sweet
    chocolate chips
  1 tablespoon margarine

Heat oven to 450°F. Allow both crust pouches to stand at room temperature 15 to 20 minutes. Remove 1 crust from pouch; unfold. Press out fold lines. If crust cracks, wet fingers and push edges together. Sprinkle 1 teaspoon flour over crust. Turn crust floured side down on ungreased cookie sheet. Using paper pattern as guide, cut crust into heart shape.* Generously prick crust with fork. Bake at 450°F. for 9 to 11 minutes or until lightly browned. Cool. Repeat with remaining crust.

In small saucepan, combine sugar, cornstarch and salt. Gradually add milk. Cook over medium heat until mixture boils and thickens, stirring constantly. Remove from heat. In small bowl, combine lemon juice and egg yolks; blend well. Add about ⅓ of the hot milk mixture to the egg yolk mixture, stirring constantly to blend.

Stir egg yolk mixture into remaining milk mixture in saucepan. Cook an additional 2 minutes, stirring constantly. DO NOT BOIL. Stir in 1 tablespoon margarine until melted. Cover; refrigerate until cool.

In small bowl, combine whipping cream and powdered sugar. Beat until stiff peaks form. Fold lemon mixture into whipped cream.

To assemble, place 1 heart-shaped pie crust on serving plate; spread with ½ of lemon filling mixture. Top with second crust and remaining filling. Arrange strawberry halves around top edge of torte ¼ inch from edge. In small saucepan, melt chocolate chips and 1 tablespoon margarine. Drizzle over lemon filling on top of torte. Refrigerate until serving time. Store any remaining torte in refrigerator. 8 to 10 servings.

TIP: *To make pattern, cut a piece of paper into a heart shape about 10½ inches high and 10 inches wide.

NUTRITION INFORMATION PER SERVING

SERVING SIZE: 1/10 OF RECIPE		PERCENT U.S. RDA PER SERVING	
CALORIES	380	PROTEIN	6%
PROTEIN	4g	VITAMIN A	10%
CARBOHYDRATE	35g	VITAMIN C	25%
FAT	25g	THIAMINE	2%
CHOLESTEROL	100mg	RIBOFLAVIN	6%
SODIUM	270mg	NIACIN	*
POTASSIUM	150mg	CALCIUM	6%
		IRON	2%

*Contains less than 2% of the U.S. RDA of this nutrient.

re is a delicious cookie version of the pular chocolate-covered cherry. The :ipe makes 4 dozen—plenty of cookies enjoy and some to keep on hand in ? freezer.

CHOCOLATE CHERRY CORDIAL COOKIES

)OKIES
- ½ cup semi-sweet chocolate chips
- ½ cup firmly packed brown sugar
- ¼ cup margarine or butter, softened
- 1 egg
- 1 cup Pillsbury's BEST® All Purpose or Unbleached Flour
- ½ teaspoon baking powder
- -oz. jar maraschino cherries, well drained, reserving 2 to 3 teaspoons liquid

?OSTING
- ½ cup semi-sweet chocolate chips
- 2 teaspoons margarine or butter

at oven to 350°F. Melt ½ cup ocolate chips in small saucepan over v heat, stirring constantly. In small wl, beat brown sugar and ¼ cup argarine until fluffy. Add egg and :lted chocolate chips; mix well. ghtly spoon flour into measuring cup; el off. Stir in flour and baking wder; mix well. For easier handling, rigerate 10 to 15 minutes.

ap 1 teaspoon dough evenly around :h cherry to completely cover. Place nch apart on ungreased cookie :ets. Bake at 350°F. for 10 to minutes or until set. Remove from okie sheets; cool completely.

r frosting, in small saucepan melt cup chocolate chips and 2 teaspoons argarine over low heat until smooth, ring constantly. Add enough erved maraschino cherry liquid until sting is of desired dipping isistency; beat until smooth. Dip s of cooled cookies in frosting. ow cookies to dry in single layer on xed paper. 4 dozen cookies.

tured top to bottom: Chocolate Cherry rdial Cookies, Chocolate Meringue ses, Glazed Brownie Hearts p. 54

HIGH ALTITUDE—Above 3500 Feet: Increase flour to 1¼ cups. Bake as directed above.

NUTRITION INFORMATION PER SERVING

SERVING SIZE: 1 COOKIE		PERCENT U.S. RDA PER SERVING	
CALORIES	60	PROTEIN	*
PROTEIN	1g	VITAMIN A	*
CARBOHYDRATE	8g	VITAMIN C	*
FAT	3g	THIAMINE	*
CHOLESTEROL	6mg	RIBOFLAVIN	*
SODIUM	20mg	NIACIN	*
POTASSIUM	25mg	CALCIUM	*
		IRON	*

*Contains less than 2% of the U.S. RDA of this nutrient.

Your sweetheart is sure to adore these light, cocoa-flavored meringue cookies with chocolate kiss centers. Bake them on parchment paper for delicate browning.

CHOCOLATE MERINGUE KISSES

- 3 egg whites
- ¼ teaspoon vinegar
- ⅛ teaspoon salt
- ¾ cup sugar
- ½ teaspoon vanilla
- 1 tablespoon unsweetened cocoa
- 48 milk chocolate kisses, unwrapped

Heat oven to 300°F. Line cookie sheets with parchment paper. In small bowl, beat egg whites, vinegar and salt until foamy. Gradually add sugar and vanilla, beating until stiff peaks form. Beat in cocoa.

Pipe or spoon batter into 1-inch mounds on parchment-lined cookie sheets. Bake at 300°F. for 15 minutes or until meringues are partially set. Place 1 chocolate kiss in center of each meringue; press down. Bake for an additional 5 to 10 minutes or until dry and edges are lightly browned. Remove from oven; cool completely. Remove from parchment paper. 4 dozen cookies.

HIGH ALTITUDE—Above 3500 Feet: Bake at 300°F. for 10 minutes. Place chocolate kisses on meringues as directed above. Bake for an additional 5 minutes.

NUTRITION INFORMATION PER SERVING

SERVING SIZE: 1 COOKIE		PERCENT U.S. RDA PER SERVING	
CALORIES	40	PROTEIN	*
PROTEIN	1g	VITAMIN A	*
CARBOHYDRATE	6g	VITAMIN C	*
FAT	1g	THIAMINE	*
CHOLESTEROL	0mg	RIBOFLAVIN	*
SODIUM	15mg	NIACIN	*
POTASSIUM	25mg	CALCIUM	*
		IRON	*

*Contains less than 2% of the U.S. RDA of this nutrient.

GLAZED BROWNIE HEARTS

BROWNIE
21½-oz. pkg. Pillsbury Fudge
Brownie Mix
½ cup water
½ cup oil
1 egg

GLAZE
4 oz. chocolate-flavored candy
coating, cut into pieces
2 teaspoons oil
4 oz. vanilla-flavored candy
coating, cut into pieces
2 teaspoons oil

The smoothest, creamiest, fudgiest no-cook candy ever—cut out with small heart-shaped cookie cutters and package brightly for your sweetheart.

PAT-IN-PAN CHOCOLATE FUDGE

½ cup margarine or butter
8-oz. pkg. cream cheese
3 oz. (3 squares) unsweetened
chocolate
6 cups powdered sugar

Line 13x9-inch pan with foil so that foil extends over sides of pan. In large saucepan, combine margarine, cream cheese and chocolate. Heat just until melted and mixture is smooth, stirring constantly. Remove from heat. Add powdered sugar, 1 cup at a time, mixing well after each addition; knead if necessary. Press mixture evenly in foil-lined pan. Refrigerate to set. Remove fudge from pan by lifting foil; remove foil from fudge. Cut into squares or desired shapes. Decorate as desired. Store in refrigerator. About 2½ pounds.

Heat oven to 350°F. Line 13x9-inch pan with foil; grease bottom. In large bowl, combine all brownie ingredients; beat 50 strokes with spoon. Spread in greased pan. Bake at 350°F. for 33 to 35 minutes or until set. DO NOT OVERBAKE. Cool completely. Freeze brownies ½ hour.

Remove brownies from pan; place on cutting board. Using 2½-inch heart-shaped cookie cutter, cut out 8 to 10 brownie hearts. In small saucepan, melt chocolate-flavored candy coating and 2 teaspoons oil over low heat, stirring occasionally until smooth; keep warm. Quickly dip sides of 4 or 5 brownies into chocolate; allow excess to drip off.

Place brownies on waxed paper. Spoon melted chocolate over tops of brownies; smooth out with knife. Repeat with vanilla-flavored candy coating, 2 teaspoons oil and remaining 4 to 5 brownies.* Drizzle small amount of contrasting chocolate randomly over each brownie. 8 to 10 brownies.

TIP: *Brownies may need to be dipped and frosted twice to completely cover with vanilla-flavored candy coating.

HIGH ALTITUDE—Above 3500 Feet: Add ¼ cup flour to dry brownie mix. Bake as directed above.

NUTRITION INFORMATION PER SERVING

SERVING SIZE: 1 OUNCE		PERCENT U.S. RDA PER SERVING	
CALORIES	110	PROTEIN	*
PROTEIN	1g	VITAMIN A	2%
CARBOHYDRATE	16g	VITAMIN C	*
FAT	5g	THIAMINE	*
CHOLESTEROL	6mg	RIBOFLAVIN	*
SODIUM	45mg	NIACIN	*
POTASSIUM	25mg	CALCIUM	*
		IRON	*

*Contains less than 2% of the U.S. RDA of this nutrient.

NUTRITION INFORMATION PER SERVING

SERVING SIZE: 1 BROWNIE		PERCENT U.S. RDA PER SERVING	
CALORIES	500	PROTEIN	6%
PROTEIN	4g	VITAMIN A	*
CARBOHYDRATE	62g	VITAMIN C	*
FAT	26g	THIAMINE	25%
CHOLESTEROL	25mg	RIBOFLAVIN	20%
SODIUM	230mg	NIACIN	6%
POTASSIUM	200mg	CALCIUM	4%
		IRON	8%

*Contains less than 2% of the U.S. RDA of this nutrient.

These treats are like the crispy cereal bars you enjoyed as a child but chocolate chips and sunflower seeds have been added. Decorate each cookie heart with maraschino cherries and add a bow or wrap it in colored cellophane for a special treat.

CHERRY NUT HEARTS

        4 cups crisp rice cereal
10½-oz. pkg. miniature
            marshmallows
        1 cup miniature semi-sweet
            chocolate chips
        ¾ cup shelled salted sunflower
            seeds
        3 tablespoons margarine or
            butter
        ½ cup maraschino cherries,
            drained and halved

Grease 13x9-inch pan; line with foil and grease again. In large bowl, combine cereal, 1 cup of the marshmallows, chocolate chips and sunflower seeds.

In medium saucepan, melt remaining marshmallows and margarine over medium heat until smooth, stirring constantly. Pour over cereal mixture; stir until well coated. With wet hands, press mixture into bottom of greased and foil-lined pan. Refrigerate until firm, about 1 hour.

Remove cereal mixture from pan by lifting the foil. Cut 4-inch heart from cardboard using pattern provided. Place cardboard heart on top of cereal mixture. Using sharp paring knife, cut around pattern to form 5 or 6 hearts. Decorate hearts with maraschino cherry halves. 5 to 6 cookies.

NUTRITION INFORMATION PER SERVING

SERVING SIZE: 1 COOKIE		PERCENT U.S. RDA PER SERVING	
CALORIES	560	PROTEIN	10%
PROTEIN	7g	VITAMIN A	20%
CARBOHYDRATE	81g	VITAMIN C	15%
FAT	24g	THIAMINE	15%
CHOLESTEROL	0mg	RIBOFLAVIN	20%
SODIUM	310mg	NIACIN	25%
POTASSIUM	250mg	CALCIUM	2%
		IRON	20%

Cherry Nut Hearts Diagram

These tender butter cookies are made special by painting on your own message or design using melted white chocolate.

CHOCOLATE SHORTBREAD HEARTS

1 cup powdered sugar
1 cup butter or margarine
½ teaspoon almond extract
1¾ cups Pillsbury's BEST® All
    Purpose or Unbleached Flour
¼ cup unsweetened cocoa

GLAZE
2 oz. (2 squares) white baking bar
2 teaspoons oil

Heat oven to 350°F. In large bowl, beat powdered sugar and butter until light and fluffy. Add almond extract; blend well. Lightly spoon flour into measuring cup; level off. Stir in flour and cocoa; mix well. Divide dough in half. On floured surface, roll out half of dough at a time, to ¼-inch thickness. Cut with floured 3-inch heart-shaped cookie cutter. Place 1 inch apart on ungreased cookie sheets. Bake at 350°F. for 8 to 11 minutes or until set. Cool 1 minute; remove from cookie sheets. Cool completely.

In small saucepan, melt white baking bar and oil over low heat, stirring constantly. Using clean small paint brush, dip brush into glaze; paint design onto cookies. 22 cookies.

HIGH ALTITUDE—Above 3500 Feet: No change.

NUTRITION INFORMATION PER SERVING

SERVING SIZE: 1 COOKIE		PERCENT U.S. RDA PER SERVING	
CALORIES	150	PROTEIN	2%
PROTEIN	1g	VITAMIN A	6%
CARBOHYDRATE	14g	VITAMIN C	*
FAT	10g	THIAMINE	4%
CHOLESTEROL	25mg	RIBOFLAVIN	2%
SODIUM	95mg	NIACIN	2%
POTASSIUM	25mg	CALCIUM	*
		IRON	2%

*Contains less than 2% of the U.S. RDA of this nutrient.

CHOCOLATE ORANGE CHEESECAKE

⅓ cup graham cracker crumb
4 (8-oz.) pkg. cream cheese, soften
1⅓ cups sugar
4 eggs
2 tablespoons orange-flavor
    liqueur or orange juice
1 teaspoon grated orange pe
3 oz. (3 squares) semi-swee
    chocolate, melted

Heat oven to 325°F. Lightly grease bottom and sides of 9-inch springforn pan. Sprinkle graham cracker crumb over bottom and sides of pan. In large bowl, beat cream cheese until light al fluffy. Gradually add sugar; beat well Add eggs, one at a time, beating well after each addition. Add liqueur and orange peel; beat 2 minutes at mediu speed, scraping sides of bowl occasionally.

In small bowl, reserve 1½ cups of batter. Pour remaining batter into crumb-lined pan. Slowly blend melte chocolate into reserved batter. Drop spoonfuls of chocolate batter onto batter in pan. Using a table knife, swi chocolate batter through light batter to marble.

Bake at 325°F. for 1 hour or until set. (To minimize cracking, place shallow pan half full of water on lower oven rack during baking.) Cool in pan. Refrigerate several hours or overnight Before serving, carefully remove side: of pan. 16 servings.

TIP: To form heart design in top of cheesecak
    spoon chocolate batter by teaspoonfuls o
    batter in pan, forming 9 drops around
    outside and 5 drops in center; continue to
    spoon batter onto drops using all of
    chocolate batter. Starting in center of 1 ou
    drop, run knife through centers of outer
    drops; run knife through centers of inner
    drops, forming 2 separate rings of
    connected hearts.

NUTRITION INFORMATION PER SERVING

SERVING SIZE: 1/16 OF RECIPE		PERCENT U.S. RDA PER SERVING	
CALORIES	330	PROTEIN	8%
PROTEIN	6g	VITAMIN A	20%
CARBOHYDRATE	24g	VITAMIN C	
FAT	23g	THIAMINE	
CHOLESTEROL	130mg	RIBOFLAVIN	10%
SODIUM	200mg	NIACIN	
POTASSIUM	110mg	CALCIUM	4%
		IRON	6%

*Contains less than 2% of the U.S. RDA of this nutrient.

Chocolate Orange Cheesec

ANYTIME TREATS

Chocolatey goodies for lunchtime, snacktime, bedtime or anytime.

For the dedicated chocolate lover, chocolate treats don't have to be sophisticated, highfalutin or elegant. They just have to be good and chocolatey. And that best describes this assortment of treats—good, chocolatey, and ready for eating.

These are the goodies you grab when you need a pick-me-up snack, when you're packing a lunch, when you're settling down to watch the late-late movie, when you want a "little something" to go with a steaming mug of coffee. They're the treats like Grandma used to make on cold, rainy days. They're bars, biscuits and breads; cupcakes, coffee cakes and cookies. They're fun to make and fun to eat.

So what could lift the spirits of a chocolate lover faster than *Double Chocolate Chunk Cupcakes*? They're so good, they don't need frosting. But go ahead, splurge and top them with a fudgy frosting if you like. Or sink your teeth into chewy *Chocolate Peanut Butter Cup Cookies* loaded with peanut butter chips and chopped up peanut butter cups. Rapture!

Pictured left to right: German Chocolate Streusel Coffee Cake p. 60, Chocolate Honey Butter p. 67

This recipe makes two scrumptious coffee cakes. Serve one warm from the oven and freeze the other to use later.

GERMAN CHOCOLATE STREUSEL COFFEE CAKE

STREUSEL

- ½ cup Pillsbury's BEST® All Purpose or Unbleached Flour
- ⅓ cup sugar
- ⅓ cup margarine or butter
- ⅓ cup chopped pecans
- ⅓ cup flaked coconut
- ⅓ cup miniature semi-sweet chocolate chips
- 2 tablespoons unsweetened cocoa
- ½ teaspoon cinnamon

COFFEE CAKE

- 1 pkg. Pillsbury Plus German Chocolate or Yellow Cake Mix
- 8-oz. carton dairy sour cream
- ¾ cup water
- 3 eggs

Heat oven to 350°F. Grease and flour two 9-inch round cake pans. Lightly spoon flour into measuring cup; level off. In large bowl, combine flour, sugar and margarine; mix with fork or pastry blender until mixture resembles coarse crumbs. Add remaining streusel ingredients; mix well. Set aside.

In large bowl, combine all cake ingredients; beat at low speed until moistened. Beat 2 minutes at highest speed. Pour 1½ cups of the batter into each greased and floured pan. Sprinkle each with about ½ cup of the streusel mixture. Bake at 350°F. for 35 to 40 minutes or until toothpick inserted in center comes out clean. Cool upright in pan 10 minutes. Invert onto large plate; invert again onto serving plate, streusel side up. Serve warm or cool. 16 servings.

HIGH ALTITUDE—Above 3500 Feet: Add ⅓ c flour to dry cake mix. Bake as directed above.

NUTRITION INFORMATION PER SERVING

SERVING SIZE: 1/16 OF RECIPE		PERCENT U.S. RDA PER SERVING	
CALORIES	290	PROTEIN	6ͨ
PROTEIN	4g	VITAMIN A	6ͨ
CARBOHYDRATE	37g	VITAMIN C	
FAT	14g	THIAMINE	8ͨ
CHOLESTEROL	60mg	RIBOFLAVIN	6ͨ
SODIUM	260mg	NIACIN	4ͨ
POTASSIUM	105mg	CALCIUM	4ͨ
		IRON	6ͨ

*Contains less than 2% of the U.S. RDA of this nutrient.

Instead of choosing between raisins or coconut, try using ½ cup of each for an interesting variation.

GERMAN CHOCOLATE CHEWS

- 1 pkg. Pillsbury Plus German Chocolate Cake Mix
- 1 cup raisins or coconut
- ⅓ cup margarine or butter, softened
- ¼ cup water
- 1 egg

Heat oven to 375°F. Lightly grease cookie sheets. In large bowl, combine all ingredients by hand, mixing well. Drop by rounded teaspoonfuls 2 inche apart onto greased cookie sheets. Bake at 375°F. for 10 to 12 minutes or until edges are set. Remove from cook sheets. Cool completely. 4 dozen cookie

TIP: If desired, cookies can be frosted with Pillsbury Frosting Supreme Ready To Spread Chocolate Fudge Frosting and sprinkled with toasted coconut.

HIGH ALTITUDE—Above 3500 Feet: No chang

NUTRITION INFORMATION PER SERVING

SERVING SIZE: 1 COOKIE		PERCENT U.S. RDA PER SERVING	
CALORIES	70	PROTEIN	*
PROTEIN	1g	VITAMIN A	*
CARBOHYDRATE	11g	VITAMIN C	*
FAT	2g	THIAMINE	2%ͦ
CHOLESTEROL	6mg	RIBOFLAVIN	*
SODIUM	80mg	NIACIN	*
POTASSIUM	35mg	CALCIUM	*
		IRON	*

*Contains less than 2% of the U.S. RDA of this nutrient.

elegant twisted shaping technique
kes this crescent roll coffee cake
que. The chocolate-covered raisin
an filling provides a wonderful eating
erience.

CHOCOLATE RAISIN CRESCENT TWIST

z. pkg. cream cheese, softened
¼ cup firmly packed brown sugar
1 egg, separated (reserving white for topping)
1 teaspoon vanilla
½ cup chopped pecans or nuts
½ cup chocolate-covered raisins
z. can Pillsbury Refrigerated Quick Crescent Dinner Rolls

PPING
2 teaspoons sugar
2 teaspoons chocolate-flavored sprinkles
Reserved egg white, slightly beaten

at oven to 325°F. In medium bowl, mbine cream cheese, brown sugar, g yolk and vanilla until smooth. Stir pecans and chocolate-covered sins.

roll dough into 2 long rectangles; mly press perforations to seal. Press roll each rectangle into a 14x5-inch ctangle. Spread half of the cream eese mixture down center of each ctangle to within 1 inch of edges. rting at longest side, roll up each ctangle; pinch long seams to seal. ace rolls side by side and 3 inches art on ungreased cookie sheet. Pinch p" ends together to seal. Loosely ist by placing right roll over left, left ll over right and right roll over left. nch "bottom" ends to seal.

mbine sugar and chocolate sprinkles. ush coffee cake with egg white; rinkle with sugar mixture. Bake at .5°F. for 25 to 35 minutes or until ep golden brown. Serve warm. Store refrigerator. 8 servings.

This pull-apart morning coffee treat is made easily with Hungry Jack® Pancake Mix. It's delicious served with whipped butter and preserves.

CHOCOLATE CHIP BUBBLE BISCUITS

2½ cups Hungry Jack® Complete or Buttermilk Pancake Mix
⅓ cup sugar
½ cup miniature semi-sweet chocolate chips
⅔ cup water
½ cup dairy sour cream
½ teaspoon vanilla

TOPPING
¼ cup sugar
3 tablespoons finely chopped walnuts
½ teaspoon cinnamon

Heat oven to 375°F. Grease 9-inch square pan. In large bowl, combine pancake mix, ⅓ cup sugar and chocolate chips; stir until just mixed. Add water, sour cream and vanilla; blend well. On well-floured surface, form dough into 16 balls. Place balls in 4 rows of 4 each in greased pan.

In small bowl, combine all topping ingredients. Sprinkle evenly over balls of dough. Bake at 375°F. for 25 to 30 minutes or until golden brown. Cool 10 minutes. Serve warm. 16 biscuits.

HIGH ALTITUDE—Above 3500 Feet: Add ¼ cup flour to dry pancake mix. Bake as directed above.

These cookies are a terrific after school snack.

COCOA-MALLOW COOKIE-WICHES

COOKIE

    1 cup sugar
    ½ cup margarine or butter, softened
    1 teaspoon vanilla
    1 egg
    1 cup milk
    2 cups Pillsbury's BEST® All Purpose or Unbleached Flour
    ½ cup unsweetened cocoa
    1½ teaspoons baking soda
    ½ teaspoon baking powder
    ½ teaspoon salt

FILLING

    2 cups powdered sugar
    1 cup marshmallow creme
    ¼ cup margarine or butter, softened
    ¼ cup shortening
    3 to 4 teaspoons milk
    1 teaspoon vanilla

Heat oven to 375°F. Grease cookie sheets. In large bowl, combine sugar, ½ cup margarine, 1 teaspoon vanilla and egg; blend well. Stir in 1 cup milk. Lightly spoon flour into measuring cup; level off. Add remaining cookie ingredients, mixing well. Drop dough by rounded teaspoonfuls 2 inches apart onto greased cookie sheets. Bake at 375°F. for 7 to 9 minutes or until edges appear set. Cool 1 minute; remove from cookie sheets. Cool.

In large bowl, combine all filling ingredients; beat until light and fluffy, about 2 minutes. Place flat sides of 2 cookies together with 1 tablespoon filling, sandwich-style. Store in tightly covered container.
30 sandwich cookies.

HIGH ALTITUDE—Above 3500 Feet: No change.

NUTRITION INFORMATION PER SERVING

SERVING SIZE: 1 COOKIE		PERCENT U.S. RDA PER SERVING	
CALORIES	170	PROTEIN	2%
PROTEIN	2g	VITAMIN A	4%
CARBOHYDRATE	24g	VITAMIN C	*
FAT	7g	THIAMINE	4%
CHOLESTEROL	10mg	RIBOFLAVIN	2%
SODIUM	170mg	NIACIN	2%
POTASSIUM	35mg	CALCIUM	2%
		IRON	2%

*Contains less than 2% of the U.S. RDA of this nutrient.

"Colorful" and "tasty" are only two words that describe this flavorful bread. Make sure to keep it tightly wrapped to maintain moistness.

SOUR CREAM CHOCOLATE CHIP DATE BREAD

    1 pkg. Pillsbury Date or Nut Quick Bread Mix
    ¾ cup water
    ½ cup dairy sour cream
    1 egg
    6-oz. pkg. (1 cup) semi-sweet chocolate chips
    ½ cup coarsely chopped maraschino cherries, well drained

Heat oven to 350°F. Grease and flour bottom only of 8x4 or 9x5-inch loaf pan. In large bowl, combine bread mix, water, sour cream and egg; stir 50 to 75 strokes until dry particles are moistened. Stir in chocolate chips and cherries; mix well. Pour into greased and floured pan.

Bake at 350°F. for 55 to 65 minutes or until toothpick inserted in center comes out clean. Cool loaf in pan on cooling rack 15 minutes; remove from pan. Cool completely before slicing. Wrap tightly; store in refrigerator.
1 (16-slice) loaf.

HIGH ALTITUDE—Above 3500 Feet: Add 2 tablespoons flour to dry bread mix. Bake at 375°F. for 50 to 60 minutes.

NUTRITION INFORMATION PER SERVING

SERVING SIZE: 1 SLICE		PERCENT U.S. RDA PER SERVING	
CALORIES	200	PROTEIN	4%
PROTEIN	2g	VITAMIN A	*
CARBOHYDRATE	32g	VITAMIN C	*
FAT	7g	THIAMINE	6%
CHOLESTEROL	20mg	RIBOFLAVIN	4%
SODIUM	115mg	NIACIN	4%
POTASSIUM	130mg	CALCIUM	2%
		IRON	6%

*Contains less than 2% of the U.S. RDA of this nutrient.

Double Chocolate Chunk Cupcakes

DOUBLE CHOCOLATE CHUNK CUPCAKES

2 cups Pillsbury's BEST® All
    Purpose or Unbleached Flour
½ cup firmly packed brown sugar
¼ cup unsweetened cocoa
1 teaspoon baking soda
¼ teaspoon salt
1 cup buttermilk*
½ cup margarine or butter, melted
½ teaspoon almond extract
1 egg
½ cup vanilla milk chips or 3 oz.
    chopped white baking bar
½ cup milk chocolate chips
¼ cup chopped slivered almonds

Heat oven to 375°F. Grease 18 muffin cups. Lightly spoon flour into measuring cup; level off. In large bowl, combine flour, brown sugar, cocoa, baking soda and salt; blend well. Add buttermilk, margarine, almond extract and egg; blend just until dry ingredients are moistened. Fold in vanilla and milk chocolate chips and almonds.

Fill greased muffin cups ¾ full. Bake at 375°F. for 15 to 20 minutes or until toothpick inserted in center comes out clean. Cool 3 minutes; remove from pan. Serve warm or cool. 18 cupcakes.

TIP: *To substitute for buttermilk, use
    1 tablespoon vinegar or lemon juice plus
    milk to make 1 cup.

HIGH ALTITUDE—Above 3500 Feet: No change.

NUTRITION INFORMATION PER SERVING

SERVING SIZE: 1 CUPCAKE		PERCENT U.S. RDA PER SERVING	
CALORIES	200	PROTEIN	6%
PROTEIN	4g	VITAMIN A	4%
CARBOHYDRATE	24g	VITAMIN C	*
FAT	10g	THIAMINE	6%
CHOLESTEROL	15mg	RIBOFLAVIN	8%
SODIUM	190mg	NIACIN	4%
POTASSIUM	120mg	CALCIUM	6%
		IRON	6%

*Contains less than 2% of the U.S. RDA of this nutrient.

Peanut butter and chocolate combined with crisp rice cereal and oats make a bar treat that puts smiles on faces of kids of all ages.

AFTER SCHOOL CRUNCH BARS

6-oz. pkg. (1 cup) semi-sweet
    chocolate chips
½ cup peanut butter chips
⅓ cup margarine
1 teaspoon vanilla
2 cups crisp rice cereal
1 cup quick-cooking rolled oats

GLAZE
¼ cup peanut butter chips
1 teaspoon oil

Grease 9-inch square or round pan. In large saucepan, melt chocolate chips, ½ cup peanut butter chips and margarine over low heat, stirring constantly until smooth. Remove from heat; stir in vanilla. Add cereal and oats; stir until well coated. Press in greased pan.

In small saucepan, melt glaze ingredients over low heat, stirring constantly until smooth. Drizzle over bars. If desired, refrigerate until set. Cut into bars. 16 bars.

▦ MICROWAVE DIRECTIONS: In medium microwave-safe bowl, combine chocolate chips, ½ cup peanut butter chips and margarine. Microwave on MEDIUM for 2 to 3 minutes, stirring once halfway through cooking. Stir until smooth. Continue as directed above. To prepare glaze, in small microwave-safe bowl, combine glaze ingredients. Microwave on MEDIUM for 1 to 2 minutes; stir until smooth. Drizzle over bars. If desired, refrigerate until set. Cut into bars.

NUTRITION INFORMATION PER SERVING

SERVING SIZE: 1 BAR		PERCENT U.S. RDA PER SERVING	
CALORIES	170	PROTEIN	4%
PROTEIN	3g	VITAMIN A	6%
CARBOHYDRATE	16g	VITAMIN C	2%
FAT	11g	THIAMINE	6%
CHOLESTEROL	0mg	RIBOFLAVIN	4%
SODIUM	105mg	NIACIN	6%
POTASSIUM	100mg	CALCIUM	*
		IRON	4%

*Contains less than 2% of the U.S. RDA of this nutrient.

Peanut butter chips and peanut butter cup candies combine in a chocolate-flavored dough for an outstanding taste sensation. We suggest taking a batch of these to the next Brownie or Cub Scout meeting.

CHOCOLATE PEANUT BUTTER CUP COOKIES

¾ cup sugar
¾ cup firmly packed brown
    sugar
1 cup margarine or butter,
    softened
¾ cup creamy peanut butter
1 teaspoon vanilla
2 eggs
2 cups Pillsbury's BEST® All
    Purpose or Unbleached
    Flour
⅓ cup unsweetened cocoa
1 teaspoon baking soda
1 teaspoon salt
6 oz. (1 cup) peanut butter
    chips
3 (1.8-oz.) pkg. milk chocolate-
    covered peanut butter
    cups, cut into pieces

Heat oven to 350°F. In large bowl, beat sugar, brown sugar, margarine and peanut butter until light and fluffy. Add vanilla and eggs; blend well. Lightly spoon flour into measuring cup; level off. Add flour, cocoa, baking soda and salt; mix well. Stir in peanut butter chips and peanut butter cup candy pieces. Drop dough by heaping teaspoonfuls 2 inches apart onto ungreased cookie sheets. Bake at 350°F for 10 to 12 minutes or until lightly browned and set. Cool 1 minute; remove from cookie sheets.
5 dozen cookies.

HIGH ALTITUDE—Above 3500 Feet: Decrease sugar to ½ cup. Increase flour to 2¼ cups. Bake as directed above.

NUTRITION INFORMATION PER SERVING

SERVING SIZE: 1 COOKIE		PERCENT U.S. RDA PER SERVING	
CALORIES	120	PROTEIN	4%
PROTEIN	2g	VITAMIN A	2%
CARBOHYDRATE	12g	VITAMIN C	*
FAT	7g	THIAMINE	2%
CHOLESTEROL	8mg	RIBOFLAVIN	2%
SODIUM	125mg	NIACIN	4%
POTASSIUM	70mg	CALCIUM	*
		IRON	2%

*Contains less than 2% of the U.S. RDA of this nutrient.

Pictured top to bottom: Chocolate Peanut Butter Cup Cookies, After School Crunch Bars

The dough for this "big batch" recipe is shaped into rolls and frozen for easier slicing. Bake half to enjoy now and freeze the rest for later.

SUGAR COOKIE CHIPPER SLICES

1 cup sugar
1 cup margarine or butter, softened
½ teaspoon almond extract
2 eggs
2 cups Pillsbury's BEST® All Purpose or Unbleached Flour
¾ cup Pillsbury's BEST® Whole Wheat Flour
1 teaspoon baking soda
12-oz. pkg. (2 cups) miniature semi-sweet chocolate chips

In large bowl, beat sugar and margarine until light and fluffy. Add almond extract and eggs; blend well. Lightly spoon flour into measuring cup; level off. Add all purpose flour, whole wheat flour and baking soda; mix well. Stir in chocolate chips. Cover; refrigerate 2 hours. Divide dough into 4 equal parts; shape each part into a roll 1½ inches in diameter. Wrap in waxed paper; freeze 1½ hours or until firm.

Heat oven to 350°F. Cut dough into ¼-inch slices. Place 1 inch apart on ungreased cookie sheets. Bake at 350°F. for 8 to 10 minutes or until very lightly browned. Cool 1 minute; remove from cookie sheets. Cool completely.
6 dozen cookies.

HIGH ALTITUDE—Above 3500 Feet: Increase whole wheat flour to 1 cup. Bake as directed above.

NUTRITION INFORMATION PER SERVING

SERVING SIZE: 1 COOKIE		PERCENT U.S. RDA PER SERVING	
CALORIES	80	PROTEIN	*
PROTEIN	1g	VITAMIN A	2%
CARBOHYDRATE	9g	VITAMIN C	*
FAT	4g	THIAMINE	2%
CHOLESTEROL	8mg	RIBOFLAVIN	*
SODIUM	45mg	NIACIN	*
POTASSIUM	25mg	CALCIUM	*
		IRON	*

*Contains less than 2% of the U.S. RDA of this nutrient.

This recipe has semi-sweet, milk and white chocolate all combined in a traditionally flavored cookie dough. It's an old favorite with some new surprises!

THREE CHIP COOKIES

¾ cup sugar
¾ cup firmly packed brown sugar
½ cup shortening
½ cup margarine or butter, softened
2 teaspoons vanilla
2 eggs
2½ cups Pillsbury's BEST® All Purpose or Unbleached Flour
1 teaspoon baking soda
½ teaspoon salt
4 oz. (¾ cup) semi-sweet chocolate chips
4 oz. (¾ cup) milk chocolate chips
4 oz. (¾ cup) vanilla milk chips or white baking bar cut into pieces
Sugar

In large bowl, beat sugar, brown sugar, shortening and margarine until light and fluffy. Add vanilla and eggs; blend well. Lightly spoon flour into measuring cup; level off. Add flour, baking soda and salt; mix well. Stir in all of the chocolate chips. Cover with plastic wrap; refrigerate 1 hour.

Heat oven to 375°F. Shape dough into 1½-inch balls. Place 2 inches apart on ungreased cookie sheets; flatten slightly with drinking glass dipped in sugar. Bake at 375°F. for 8 to 10 minutes or until golden brown. Cool 1 minute; remove from cookie sheets.
3 dozen cookies.

HIGH ALTITUDE—Above 3500 Feet: Increase flour to 3 cups. Bake as directed above.

NUTRITION INFORMATION PER SERVING

SERVING SIZE: 1 COOKIE		PERCENT U.S. RDA PER SERVING	
CALORIES	180	PROTEIN	2%
PROTEIN	2g	VITAMIN A	2%
CARBOHYDRATE	22g	VITAMIN C	*
FAT	9g	THIAMINE	4%
CHOLESTEROL	15mg	RIBOFLAVIN	4%
SODIUM	105mg	NIACIN	2%
POTASSIUM	65mg	CALCIUM	2%
		IRON	4%

*Contains less than 2% of the U.S. RDA of this nutrient.

Serve this delicious cocoa-flavored bread with Chocolate Honey Butter (this page).

BUTTERMILK CHOCOLATE BREAD

1 cup sugar
½ cup margarine or butter, softened
2 eggs
1 cup buttermilk*
1¾ cups Pillsbury's BEST® All Purpose or Unbleached Flour
½ cup unsweetened cocoa
½ teaspoon baking powder
½ teaspoon baking soda
½ teaspoon salt
⅓ cup chopped nuts

Heat oven to 350°F. Grease bottom only of 8x4 or 9x5-inch loaf pan. In large bowl, combine sugar and margarine; blend thoroughly. Add eggs; mix well. Stir in buttermilk. Lightly spoon flour into measuring cup; level off. Add flour, cocoa, baking powder, baking soda and salt. Stir just until dry particles are moistened. Stir in nuts. Pour into greased pan. Bake at 350°F. for 55 to 65 minutes or until toothpick inserted in center comes out clean. Cool in pan 15 minutes. Remove from pan; cool completely before slicing. 12 servings.

TIP: *To substitute for buttermilk, use 1 tablespoon vinegar or lemon juice plus milk to make 1 cup.

HIGH ALTITUDE—Above 3500 Feet: Increase flour to 1¾ cups plus 1 tablespoon. Bake at 375°F. for 50 to 55 minutes.

NUTRITION INFORMATION PER SERVING

SERVING SIZE: /12 OF RECIPE		PERCENT U.S. RDA PER SERVING	
CALORIES	260	PROTEIN	6%
PROTEIN	5g	VITAMIN A	6%
CARBOHYDRATE	34g	VITAMIN C	*
FAT	12g	THIAMINE	10%
CHOLESTEROL	45mg	RIBOFLAVIN	8%
SODIUM	300mg	NIACIN	6%
POTASSIUM	105mg	CALCIUM	4%
		IRON	8%

*Contains less than 2% of the U.S. RDA of this nutrient.

Serve on Buttermilk Chocolate Bread (this page) or spread on thin sugar cookies as an interesting dessert.

CHOCOLATE HONEY BUTTER

½ cup butter or margarine, softened
2 tablespoons honey
2 tablespoons chocolate-flavored syrup

In small bowl, combine all ingredients. Beat at highest speed until light and fluffy. 1 cup.

NUTRITION INFORMATION PER SERVING

SERVING SIZE: 1 TABLESPOON		PERCENT U.S. RDA PER SERVING	
CALORIES	70	PROTEIN	*
PROTEIN	0g	VITAMIN A	4%
CARBOHYDRATE	4g	VITAMIN C	*
FAT	6g	THIAMINE	*
CHOLESTEROL	15mg	RIBOFLAVIN	*
SODIUM	60mg	NIACIN	*
POTASSIUM	10mg	CALCIUM	*
		IRON	*

*Contains less than 2% of the U.S. RDA of this nutrient.

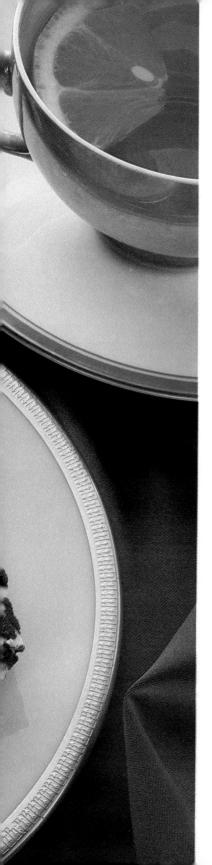

Cake mix makes a delicious base and topping for these lemony cheesecake bars. Serve with freshly brewed coffee garnished with a twist of lemon.

CHOCOLATE LEMON CREAM BARS

BASE

1 pkg.	Pillsbury Plus Devil's Food Cake Mix
½ cup	margarine or butter, softened
1	egg
½ cup	chopped walnuts

FILLING

8-oz. pkg.	cream cheese, softened
14-oz. can	sweetened condensed milk (not evaporated)
3 tablespoons	lemon juice
1 tablespoon	grated lemon peel
1	egg

Heat oven to 350°F. Grease 13x9-inch pan. In large bowl, combine cake mix, margarine and egg; mix at low speed until combined. Stir in walnuts. Reserve 1½ cups for topping; set aside. Press remaining mixture in bottom of greased pan. Bake at 350°F. for 10 minutes; cool 5 minutes.

Beat cream cheese in medium bowl until light and fluffy. Add remaining filling ingredients and beat at medium speed until smooth. Pour evenly over partially baked crust; sprinkle with reserved topping. Bake at 350°F. for an additional 20 to 25 minutes or until center is set. Cool completely. Cut into bars. Store in refrigerator. 36 bars.

HIGH ALTITUDE—Above 3500 Feet: No change.

NUTRITION INFORMATION PER SERVING

SERVING SIZE: 1 BAR		PERCENT U.S. RDA PER SERVING	
CALORIES	170	PROTEIN	4%
PROTEIN	3g	VITAMIN A	4%
CARBOHYDRATE	19g	VITAMIN C	*
FAT	9g	THIAMINE	2%
CHOLESTEROL	25mg	RIBOFLAVIN	6%
SODIUM	180mg	NIACIN	*
POTASSIUM	130mg	CALCIUM	8%
		IRON	2%

*Contains less than 2% of the U.S. RDA of this nutrient.

Chocolate Lemon Cream Bars

Having friends over for Saturday breakfast? Serve these muffins warm from the oven.

CHOCOLATE CHIP MACADAMIA NUT MUFFINS

STREUSEL

¼ cup flour
¼ cup firmly packed brown sugar
2 tablespoons margarine or butter

MUFFINS

2 cups Pillsbury's BEST® All
    Purpose or Unbleached Flour
½ cup sugar
1 teaspoon baking powder
½ teaspoon baking soda
½ teaspoon salt
¾ cup dairy sour cream
½ cup margarine or butter, melted
¼ cup milk
1 tablespoon vanilla
1 egg
½ cup chopped macadamia nuts
½ cup miniature semi-sweet
    chocolate chips

Heat oven to 375°F. Grease 18 muffin cups or line with paper baking cups. In small bowl, combine all streusel ingredients; blend with fork until mixture resembles coarse crumbs. Set aside.

Lightly spoon flour into measuring cup; level off. In large bowl, combine 2 cups flour, sugar, baking powder, baking soda and salt; blend well. Add sour cream, ½ cup margarine, milk, vanilla and egg; stir just until dry particles are moistened. Fold in macadamia nuts and chocolate chips. Fill greased or paper-lined muffin cups ¾ full; sprinkle each with 1½ teaspoons streusel. Bake at 375°F. for 18 to 20 minutes or until toothpick inserted in center comes out clean. Remove from muffin cups immediately. Serve warm. 18 muffins.

HIGH ALTITUDE—Above 3500 Feet: Increase flour to 2 cups plus 2 tablespoons. Bake as directed above.

NUTRITION INFORMATION PER SERVING

SERVING SIZE: 1 MUFFIN		PERCENT U.S. RDA PER SERVING	
CALORIES	220	PROTEIN	4%
PROTEIN	3g	VITAMIN A	6%
CARBOHYDRATE	24g	VITAMIN C	*
FAT	13g	THIAMINE	8%
CHOLESTEROL	20mg	RIBOFLAVIN	6%
SODIUM	190mg	NIACIN	4%
POTASSIUM	80mg	CALCIUM	4%
		IRON	6%

*Contains less than 2% of the U.S. RDA of this nutrient.

COOK'S NOTE

CHOCOLATE STORAGE

Store chocolate in a dry cool place, about 60 to 70°F. If the temperature is higher than 78°F. or the humidity is above 50%, chocolate should be stored in a moisture-tight container or wrapped in moisture-proof wrap. When chocolate is stored above 78°F., the cocoa butter will rise to the surface, forming "bloom" which is a dull gray discoloration. "Bloom" does not affect the flavor or quality of the chocolate when it is used in a recipe.

Because they need no rolling, you can make these scone drops even when you are in a time crunch. Top them with butter and turn a dreary winter morning into a special day.

MINI-CHIP ORANGE SCONE DROPS

SCONES

2 cups Pillsbury's BEST® All Purpose or Unbleached Flour
⅓ cup sugar
2 teaspoons baking powder
½ teaspoon salt
¼ teaspoon baking soda
⅓ cup margarine or butter
⅓ cup orange juice
⅓ cup milk
2 tablespoons grated orange peel
½ cup miniature semi-sweet chocolate chips

TOPPING

3 tablespoons sugar
½ teaspoon cinnamon

Heat oven to 375°F. Grease cookie sheets. Lightly spoon flour into measuring cup; level off. In large bowl, combine flour, ⅓ cup sugar, baking powder, salt and baking soda; blend well. Using fork or pastry blender, cut in margarine until mixture resembles coarse crumbs. Add orange juice, milk and orange peel. Stir just until dry ingredients are moistened. Stir in chocolate chips. Drop by heaping teaspoonfuls 2 inches apart onto greased cookie sheets.

In small bowl, combine topping ingredients; sprinkle over scones. Bake at 375°F. for 8 to 10 minutes or until light golden brown. Immediately remove from cookie sheets. Serve warm. 2½ dozen scones.

HIGH ALTITUDE—Above 3500 Feet: No change.

NUTRITION INFORMATION PER SERVING

SERVING SIZE: 1 SCONE		PERCENT U.S. RDA PER SERVING	
CALORIES	80	PROTEIN	*
PROTEIN	1g	VITAMIN A	*
CARBOHYDRATE	12g	VITAMIN C	2%
FAT	3g	THIAMINE	4%
CHOLESTEROL	0mg	RIBOFLAVIN	2%
SODIUM	90mg	NIACIN	2%
POTASSIUM	30mg	CALCIUM	2%
		IRON	2%

*Contains less than 2% of the U.S. RDA of this nutrient.

This banana cake can double as a snack or dessert. Keep it well covered to retain the moist texture.

CHIPPER SNACKING CAKE

¾ cup wheat germ
½ cup quick-cooking rolled oats
1 cup buttermilk*
1 cup (3 medium) mashed ripe bananas
¾ cup sugar
½ cup oil
1 teaspoon vanilla
2 eggs
1 cup Pillsbury's BEST® All Purpose or Unbleached Flour
¾ cup Pillsbury's BEST® Whole Wheat Flour
1½ teaspoons baking soda
1 teaspoon cinnamon
½ teaspoon salt
½ cup miniature semi-sweet chocolate chips
Powdered sugar

Heat oven to 350°F. Grease 13x9-inch pan. In large bowl, combine wheat germ, oats and buttermilk. Allow to stand 15 minutes. Add bananas, sugar, oil, vanilla and eggs; blend well. Lightly spoon flour into measuring cup; level off. Add all purpose and whole wheat flours, baking soda, cinnamon and salt; blend well. Fold in chocolate chips. Pour into greased pan. Bake at 350°F. for 25 to 30 minutes or until toothpick inserted in center comes out clean. Cool completely. Sprinkle with powdered sugar. 15 servings.

TIP: *To substitute for buttermilk, use 1 tablespoon vinegar or lemon juice plus milk to make 1 cup.

HIGH ALTITUDE—Above 3500 Feet: Bake at 375°F. for 20 to 25 minutes.

NUTRITION INFORMATION PER SERVING

SERVING SIZE: 1/15 OF RECIPE		PERCENT U.S. RDA PER SERVING	
CALORIES	250	PROTEIN	8%
PROTEIN	5g	VITAMIN A	*
CARBOHYDRATE	33g	VITAMIN C	*
FAT	11g	THIAMINE	15%
CHOLESTEROL	35mg	RIBOFLAVIN	8%
SODIUM	210mg	NIACIN	4%
POTASSIUM	190mg	CALCIUM	2%
		IRON	8%

*Contains less than 2% of the U.S. RDA of this nutrient.

cuit dough is wrapped around milk
)colate kisses to create this unique
l-apart coffee cake. A sugar-
namon topping bakes into a
uthwatering glaze.

CHOCOLATE SURPRISE BISCUIT RING

10-oz.) cans Hungry Jack®
    Refrigerated Flaky
    Biscuits
  20 milk chocolate candy
    kisses, unwrapped
  ½ cup sugar
  ½ teaspoon cinnamon
  ¼ cup margarine or butter,
    melted

at oven to 375°F. Generously grease
cup fluted tube pan. Separate dough
) 20 biscuits. Press or roll each
cuit to form a 2½ to 3-inch circle.
ce a chocolate kiss, point side up, on
ter of each circle. Fold dough over
s, covering completely and forming a
l; pinch edges to seal.

small bowl, combine sugar and
namon. Dip each ball into melted
rgarine; roll in sugar-cinnamon
xture. Gently place coated balls in
ased tube pan, placing seams toward
ter. Sprinkle with any remaining
ar-cinnamon mixture; drizzle with
aining margarine. Bake at 375°F. for
to 35 minutes or until golden
wn. Cool 1 minute; remove from
. Serve warm. 10 servings.

RITION INFORMATION PER SERVING

ING SIZE: OF RECIPE		PERCENT U.S. RDA PER SERVING	
RIES	310	PROTEIN	6%
EIN	4g	VITAMIN A	4%
OHYDRATE	39g	VITAMIN C	*
	15g	THIAMINE	10%
LESTEROL	0mg	RIBOFLAVIN	10%
UM	660mg	NIACIN	8%
SSIUM	75mg	CALCIUM	2%
		IRON	8%

tains less than 2% of the U.S. RDA of this nutrient.

colate Surprise Biscuit Ring

Remember the old-fashioned date bars
your grandma made? The base and
topping of those date bars is made
quicker using cake mix. Adding
chocolate to the date filling creates an
outstanding flavor.

CHOCOLATE DATE BARS

FILLING
8-oz. pkg. chopped dates
  ¼ cup sugar
  ¾ cup water
  1 oz. (1 square) unsweetened
    chocolate

BASE
  1 pkg. Pillsbury Plus Yellow Cake
    Mix
  1 cup quick-cooking rolled oats
  ½ cup margarine or butter,
    softened
  1 egg

Heat oven to 350°F. Grease 13x9-inch
pan. In medium saucepan, combine
dates, sugar and water. Bring mixture
to a boil; reduce heat to low. Add
chocolate; continue cooking until
mixture thickens, stirring constantly.
Remove from heat; set aside.

In large bowl, combine cake mix, oats
and margarine at low speed until
crumbly. Reserve 1 cup crumbs for
topping. Blend egg into remaining
crumb mixture; press in greased pan.
Bake at 350°F. for 12 to 15 minutes
or until light golden brown.
Cool 10 minutes.

Spread date mixture over cooled base;
sprinkle with reserved crumb mixture.
Bake at 350°F. for an additional 20 to
25 minutes. Cool completely. Cut into
bars. 36 bars.

HIGH ALTITUDE—Above 3500 Feet: No change.

NUTRITION INFORMATION PER SERVING

SERVING SIZE: 1 BAR		PERCENT U.S. RDA PER SERVING	
CALORIES	120	PROTEIN	2%
PROTEIN	1g	VITAMIN A	2%
CARBOHYDRATE	19g	VITAMIN C	*
FAT	5g	THIAMINE	4%
CHOLESTEROL	8mg	RIBOFLAVIN	2%
SODIUM	120mg	NIACIN	2%
POTASSIUM	65mg	CALCIUM	2%
		IRON	2%

*Contains less than 2% of the U.S. RDA of this nutrient.

CHOCOLATE— NOW!

Quiet your chocolate cravings with these clever creations.

When only chocolate will do, when you just can't wait, when you need chocolate and you need it NOW, don't just grab a handful of chocolate chips or stir up a glass of chocolate milk. Try these quick fixes that are guaranteed to quiet your cravings— pronto.

What makes them such a cinch are simple ingredients, and recruiting your microwave to marvelously melt chocolate in mere minutes.

Some selections are downright elegant candies suitable for gift-giving or desserts destined for dinner guests. Others are a boon for after-school snacks with some that kids can make on their own.

When the spirit moves you, lounge on the sofa and nibble bonbons, **Filled Chocolate Cup Candies** or **Dipped Peppermint Creams.** Cream cheese and orange marmalade nestle at the center of the filled cups, and crushed peppermint candies fleck the chocolate-dipped squares. Both are made easier with your microwave, but also can be prepared quickly on top of your range.

A blazing campfire isn't necessary to fix S'mores anymore. Just pop marshmallows mounted on squares of milk chocolate bars and graham crackers into a microwave. In seconds, you'll create the treat that kids and grownups can eat a million of and still come back for "some more."

Pictured top to bottom: Marble Peanut Bark p. 77, Choco-Caramel Nut Puddles p. 76

These easy but elegant chocolate confections look just like they came from your favorite candy shop. Top them with dried fruits and your choice of nuts.

CHOCO-CARAMEL NUT PUDDLES

 4 oz. milk chocolate, cut into pieces
 4 oz. chocolate-flavored candy
     coating, cut into pieces
10 caramels, unwrapped
 2 teaspoons milk
    Dried quartered apricots
    Pecan halves
    Raisins
    Whole blanched almonds

Using pencil, draw thirty-six 1½-inch circles on waxed paper-lined cookie sheets, 2 inches apart. In medium heavy saucepan, melt milk chocolate and chocolate-flavored candy coating over low heat until smooth, stirring constantly. Spoon and spread 1 tablespoon chocolate mixture onto each circle. Refrigerate about 10 minutes or until chocolate is set.

In small saucepan, melt caramels and milk over low heat until smooth, stirring constantly. Spoon about ½ teaspoon caramel mixture onto each chocolate circle, leaving ½ inch chocolate showing around edge.

Decorate with combinations of dried fruits and nuts; press down lightly. Refrigerate until set. Gently remove candies from waxed paper. Store in single layer in airtight container. 2 dozen candies.

MICROWAVE DIRECTIONS: Dra circles as directed above. In medium microwave-safe bowl, combine milk chocolate and chocolate-flavored cand coating. Microwave on MEDIUM for 3 to 4 minutes, stirring once halfway through cooking. Stir until smooth. Spoon and spread 1 tablespoon chocolate mixture onto each circle. Refrigerate about 10 minutes or until chocolate is set. In small microwave-safe bowl, combine caramels and milk Microwave on MEDIUM for 2½ to 3 minutes, stirring once every minute until melted. Stir until smooth. Continue as directed above.

NUTRITION INFORMATION PER SERVING

SERVING SIZE: 1 CANDY		PERCENT U.S. RDA PER SERVING	
CALORIES	80	PROTEIN	*
PROTEIN	1g	VITAMIN A	*
CARBOHYDRATE	9g	VITAMIN C	*
FAT	4g	THIAMINE	2%
CHOLESTEROL	0mg	RIBOFLAVIN	4%
SODIUM	15mg	NIACIN	*
POTASSIUM	55mg	CALCIUM	2%
		IRON	*

*Contains less than 2% of the U.S. RDA of this nutrient.

COOK'S NOTE

MELTING CHOCOLATE IN THE MICROWAVE

Place chopped or grated chocolate in an uncovered microwave-safe bowl or dish. Microwave on MEDIUM, stirring once every minute until chocolate is melted. Stir until smooth. This method can be repeated if chocolate cools and hardens.

...ese candies will look store-bought ...en you are finished. Make the candy ...en easier by melting the chocolate in ...e microwave.

FILLED CHOCOLATE CUP CANDIES

...2-oz. pkg. (2 cups) milk chocolate
    chips
  2 tablespoons shortening
 36 miniature paper or foil baking
    cups
  4 oz. cream cheese, softened
 ¼ cup orange marmalade
  2 tablespoons powdered sugar

... small heavy saucepan, melt milk ...ocolate chips and shortening over ...w heat until smooth, stirring ...nstantly; keep warm. Spoon ...aspoonful melted chocolate into ...iniature baking cup; rotate cup in ...lm of hand to coat sides with ...ocolate. Place on tray; repeat for ...maining cups. Reserve remaining ...elted chocolate. Refrigerate chocolate ...ps 5 minutes or until firm.

...eanwhile, in small bowl combine ...eam cheese, orange marmalade and ...owdered sugar; beat until smooth. ...oon about 1 teaspoon filling into ...ch cup; spoon ½ teaspoon reserved ...elted chocolate over filling to cover ...mpletely. Refrigerate until candy is ...t. 36 candies.

MICROWAVE DIRECTIONS: In ...edium microwave-safe bowl, melt ...ilk chocolate chips and shortening on ...EDIUM for 3 to 4 minutes, stirring ...ce halfway through cooking. Stir ...til smooth. Continue as directed ...ove.

This is an irresistible combination of white and milk chocolate swirled together and sprinkled with peanuts. For best results, keep it refrigerated.

MARBLE PEANUT BARK

  6 oz. (1 cup) milk chocolate chips
  6 oz. (1 cup) vanilla milk chips or
    vanilla-flavored candy coating,
    cut into pieces
 ½ cup coarsely chopped salted
    peanuts

Line 13x9-inch pan with foil. Melt milk chocolate chips in small saucepan over very low heat, stirring constantly until smooth. Keep warm. Melt vanilla milk chips in another small saucepan over low heat, stirring constantly. Pour melted milk chocolate in foil-lined pan to evenly cover bottom. Sprinkle with peanuts. Pour melted vanilla milk chips over milk chocolate. Swirl chocolates together using tip of table knife. Refrigerate 1 hour or until firm. Break into pieces. Store in covered container in refrigerator. 14 ounces.

MICROWAVE DIRECTIONS: In small microwave-safe bowl, microwave milk chocolate chips on MEDIUM for 2½ to 3 minutes, stirring once halfway through melting. Stir until smooth. In another small microwave-safe bowl, microwave vanilla milk chips on MEDIUM for 2½ to 3 minutes, stirring once halfway through melting. Stir until smooth. Continue as directed above.

For a little added crunch, sprinkle these
treats with chopped peanuts before the
chocolate sets.

PEANUT CRACKER DIPPERS

  8 oz. chocolate-flavored candy
     coating, cut into pieces
 48 round buttery crackers
 ½ cup peanut butter

Melt chocolate coating in medium
saucepan over low heat, stirring
constantly. Using half of the crackers,
spread 1 teaspoon peanut butter on
each; top with another cracker. Using
tongs or 2 forks, dip each cookie into
chocolate. Place on wire rack over
waxed paper. Cool completely.
24 cookies.

MICROWAVE DIRECTIONS: Place
chocolate coating in medium
microwave-safe bowl. Microwave on
HIGH for 3 to 4½ minutes or until
melted, stirring every minute. Continue
as directed above.

TIP: If desired, top peanut butter layer with
raisins or coconut.

NUTRITION INFORMATION PER SERVING
SERVING SIZE:
1 COOKIE

		PERCENT U.S. RDA PER SERVING	
CALORIES	120	PROTEIN	2%
PROTEIN	2g	VITAMIN A	*
CARBOHYDRATE	11g	VITAMIN C	*
FAT	8g	THIAMINE	8%
CHOLESTEROL	0mg	RIBOFLAVIN	6%
SODIUM	105mg	NIACIN	4%
POTASSIUM	65mg	CALCIUM	2%
		IRON	*

*Contains less than 2% of the U.S. RDA of this nutrient.

Kids will enjoy making these candy
creations for friends and family.

CHOCOLATE-COVERED MARSHMALLOWS

10-oz. pkg. marshmallows (not
    miniature)
 40 toothpicks
  1 can Pillsbury Frosting
    Supreme Ready To Spread
    Chocolate Fudge Frosting
  1 cup finely chopped peanuts

Secure each marshmallow on
toothpick. In medium saucepan, warm
frosting over low heat until softened
but not runny. Dip marshmallow in
frosting to coat, wiping off excess on
inside of pan. Let dry slightly; dip
bottom half of each marshmallow in
peanuts. Set peanut side down on
waxed paper to set. Remove toothpicks.
40 candies.

NUTRITION INFORMATION PER SERVING
SERVING SIZE:
1 CANDY

		PERCENT U.S. RDA PER SERVING	
CALORIES	90	PROTEIN	*
PROTEIN	1g	VITAMIN A	*
CARBOHYDRATE	14g	VITAMIN C	*
FAT	4g	THIAMINE	*
CHOLESTEROL	0mg	RIBOFLAVIN	*
SODIUM	55mg	NIACIN	2%
POTASSIUM	50mg	CALCIUM	*
		IRON	*

*Contains less than 2% of the U.S. RDA of this nutrient.

*Pictured top to bottom: Chocolate-Covered
Marshmallows, Peanut Cracker Dippers*

Once you start eating these cereal, candy and peanut treats, you won't be able to resist them.

CHOCO-PEANUT CEREAL TREATS

6 cups chocolate-flavor frosted
corn puff cereal
8-oz. pkg. candy-coated peanut
butter pieces
½ cup salted peanuts
¼ cup margarine or butter
2 oz. (2 squares) semi-sweet
chocolate
10½-oz. pkg. miniature
marshmallows

▦ MICROWAVE DIRECTIONS:
Grease 13x9-inch pan. In large bowl,
combine cereal, peanut butter pieces
and peanuts; blend well. In large
microwave-safe bowl, combine
margarine and chocolate. Microwave on
MEDIUM for 1½ to 2 minutes, stirring
once halfway through melting. Stir
until smooth. Stir in marshmallows;
blend well. Microwave on HIGH for
1 to 2 minutes, stirring after 1 minute.
Stir until smooth. Pour chocolate-
marshmallow mixture over cereal
mixture; stir quickly to coat. With wet
hands, press into greased pan; cool.
Cut into bars. 40 bars.

NUTRITION INFORMATION PER SERVING

SERVING SIZE: 1 BAR		PERCENT U.S. RDA PER SERVING	
CALORIES	100	PROTEIN	2%
PROTEIN	2g	VITAMIN A	*
CARBOHYDRATE	14g	VITAMIN C	2%
FAT	4g	THIAMINE	4%
CHOLESTEROL	0mg	RIBOFLAVIN	4%
SODIUM	85mg	NIACIN	8%
POTASSIUM	55mg	CALCIUM	*
		IRON	6%

*Contains less than 2% of the U.S. RDA of this nutrient.

This is a great-tasting homemade version of the chewy chocolate roll candy! It's foolproof whether made on the stovetop or in the microwave.

CHEWY CHOCOLATE TOOTSIES

1 oz. (1 square) unsweetened
chocolate
1 tablespoon margarine or butter
¼ cup light corn syrup
½ teaspoon vanilla
1⅓ cups powdered sugar
¼ cup graham cracker crumbs
½ cup finely chopped walnuts

In medium saucepan, melt chocolate
and margarine over low heat, stirring
constantly. Stir in corn syrup and
vanilla; blend until smooth. Add 1 cup
powdered sugar and graham cracker
crumbs; blend well. Turn mixture out
onto waxed paper; knead in remaining
powdered sugar and walnuts. Divide
mixture into 4 equal parts. Roll each
part into 10-inch log. Cut each log into
10 equal pieces. Wrap each piece
individually in waxed paper or plastic
wrap. 40 candies.

▦ MICROWAVE DIRECTIONS: In
4-cup microwave-safe measuring cup,
microwave chocolate and margarine on
HIGH for 1 minute or until melted. Stir
until smooth. Add corn syrup and
vanilla. Microwave on HIGH for
1 minute; stir until smooth. Continue
as directed above.

NUTRITION INFORMATION PER SERVING

SERVING SIZE: 1 CANDY		PERCENT U.S. RDA PER SERVING	
CALORIES	40	PROTEIN	*
PROTEIN	0g	VITAMIN A	*
CARBOHYDRATE	6g	VITAMIN C	*
FAT	2g	THIAMINE	*
CHOLESTEROL	0mg	RIBOFLAVIN	*
SODIUM	10mg	NIACIN	*
POTASSIUM	15mg	CALCIUM	*
		IRON	*

*Contains less than 2% of the U.S. RDA of this nutrient.

...cookie-candy combination, this easy-to-make treat has a delicate rich flavor without being overly sweet. Serve in colored foil candy papers for a special touch.

MANDARIN ORANGE TRUFFLE COOKIES

11-oz. can mandarin orange
    segments, drained
6-oz. pkg. (1 cup) semi-sweet
    chocolate chips
¼ cup whipping cream or
    evaporated milk
3 tablespoons butter
12-oz. box vanilla wafers, crushed
    (3 cups)
½ cup powdered sugar
½ cup ground almonds
2 tablespoons orange-flavored
    liqueur
¾ cup chocolate-flavored
    sprinkles

In blender container or food processor bowl with metal blade, chop oranges very fine. In heavy saucepan, combine oranges, chocolate chips, cream and butter. Heat over low heat until chocolate melts, stirring constantly. Cook 5 minutes longer, stirring occasionally. Stir in cookie crumbs, sugar, almonds and liqueur. Refrigerate 30 minutes or until mixture is firm enough to handle. Shape into 1-inch balls; roll in chocolate sprinkles. To store, place in tightly covered container; refrigerate.
4½ dozen cookies.

MICROWAVE DIRECTIONS:
Chop oranges as directed above. In medium microwave-safe bowl, combine oranges, chocolate chips, cream and butter. Microwave on HIGH for 3 minutes or until chocolate melts, stirring twice during cooking. Continue as directed above.

There's no end to the variety of flavors you can make. To make it even more chocolaty, why not try using chocolate ice cream?

YOUR FAVORITE FROSTY

2 cups vanilla ice cream, slightly
    softened
Choose any 1 of the following:
    2 oz. favorite candy bar, broken
      into pieces
    ⅓ cup miniature chocolate-
      covered mint patties
    ¼ cup candy-coated chocolate or
      peanut butter pieces
    30 malted milk balls

In blender container or food processor bowl with metal blade, combine ice cream and any one of the candies listed above. Cover; blend until of desired consistency. Serve immediately.
2 (1-cup) servings.

*n-loving kids of all ages will enjoy
aking this campfire favorite in the
crowave. For best results, microwave
e S'mores on paper towels.*

MICROWAVE S'MORES

12 graham cracker squares
(1.65-oz.) milk chocolate bars
6 large marshmallows

▣ MICROWAVE DIRECTIONS: Place
chocolate bar on 1 graham cracker
uare; top with 1 marshmallow. Place
paper towel. Microwave on HIGH
10 to 15 seconds or until
arshmallow is puffed. Remove from
en and top with second graham
cker square; press down gently.
peat with remaining ingredients.
ervings.

P: For a special S'more, spread 2 teaspoons
peanut butter on graham cracker square
before adding chocolate bar.

TRITION INFORMATION PER SERVING

VING SIZE: OF RECIPE		PERCENT U.S. RDA PER SERVING	
.ORIES	160	PROTEIN	4%
TEIN	2g	VITAMIN A	*
RBOHYDRATE	25g	VITAMIN C	*
	6g	THIAMINE	*
)LESTEROL	2mg	RIBOFLAVIN	8%
)IUM	115mg	NIACIN	2%
ASSIUM	115mg	CALCIUM	4%
		IRON	4%

ntains less than 2% of the U.S. RDA of this nutrient.

*is is a unique candy with a pastry
st bottom. To save time, melt the
amels in the microwave.*

CARAMEL CANDY TOPPERS

-oz. pkg. Pillsbury All Ready Pie
Crusts
28 caramels, unwrapped
1 tablespoon milk
¼ cup margarine or butter
1 cup powdered sugar
¾ cup chopped walnuts

PPING
½ cup semi-sweet chocolate
chips
1 tablespoon shortening

Heat oven to 450°F. Allow both crust
pouches to stand at room temperature
for 15 to 20 minutes. Using 2-inch
round cookie cutter, cut 25 circles from
each crust. Place 1 inch apart on
ungreased cookie sheets; prick with
fork. Bake at 450°F. for 7 to 8 minutes
or until lightly browned. Remove to
cooling rack; cool completely.

In small saucepan, melt caramels, milk
and margarine over low heat until
smooth, stirring constantly. Stir in
powdered sugar and walnuts. Spoon
1 teaspoon caramel mixture on top of
each cooled pastry circle.

In small saucepan, melt chocolate chips
and shortening over low heat until
smooth, stirring constantly. Drizzle
chocolate over caramel layer. Allow to
set in single layer on waxed paper. Store
in tightly covered container. 50 candies.

▤ MICROWAVE DIRECTIONS:
Prepare pastry as directed above. In
medium microwave-safe bowl, combine
caramels, milk and margarine.
Microwave on MEDIUM for 3½ to
4½ minutes, stirring once every minute
until melted. Stir until smooth. Stir in
powdered sugar and walnuts. Spoon
1 teaspoon caramel mixture on top of
each cooled pastry circle. For topping,
combine chocolate chips and
shortening in small microwave-safe
bowl. Microwave on MEDIUM for 2 to
3 minutes or until melted. Stir until
smooth. Continue as directed above.

NUTRITION INFORMATION PER SERVING

SERVING SIZE: 1 CANDY		PERCENT U.S. RDA PER SERVING	
CALORIES	100	PROTEIN	*
PROTEIN	1g	VITAMIN A	*
CARBOHYDRATE	11g	VITAMIN C	*
FAT	6g	THIAMINE	*
CHOLESTEROL	2mg	RIBOFLAVIN	*
SODIUM	55mg	NIACIN	*
POTASSIUM	30mg	CALCIUM	*
		IRON	*

*Contains less than 2% of the U.S. RDA of this nutrient.

crowave S'Mores

CHOCOLATE—NOW!

Everyone loves pizza—this candy version will especially delight chocolate lovers.

CHOCOLATE CANDY PIZZA

12-oz. pkg. semi-sweet chocolate chips
6 oz. almond bark or vanilla-flavored candy coating, cut into pieces
1 cup crisp rice cereal
½ cup dry roasted peanuts
3 large red gumdrops, quartered*
3 large green gumdrops, quartered*
2 oz. almond bark or vanilla-flavored candy coating, cut into pieces

▣ MICROWAVE DIRECTIONS:
Grease 12-inch pizza pan with butter or line with foil. In 2½-quart microwave-safe bowl or 8-cup microwave-safe measuring cup, combine chocolate chips and 6 oz. almond bark. Microwave on MEDIUM for 4 to 5½ minutes or until melted, stirring twice during cooking. Stir until smooth. Stir in cereal and peanuts. Spread in buttered pan; dot with gumdrop pieces.

Place remaining 2 oz. almond bark in small microwave-safe bowl. Microwave on MEDIUM for 1 to 1¼ minutes, stirring once during cooking. Stir until smooth. Drizzle over top of pizza. Cover; store in refrigerator. Cut into wedges. 10 wedges.

CONVENTIONAL DIRECTIONS:
Prepare pan as directed above. In medium saucepan over low heat, melt chocolate chips and 6 oz. almond bark stirring constantly. Stir in cereal and peanuts. Spread in buttered pan; dot with gumdrop pieces. Melt remaining 2 oz. almond bark in small saucepan over low heat, stirring constantly until smooth. Drizzle over top of pizza. Cover; store in refrigerator. Cut into wedges.

TIP: *Other candies can be substituted.

NUTRITION INFORMATION PER SERVING

SERVING SIZE: 1 WEDGE		PERCENT U.S. RDA PER SERVING	
CALORIES	380	PROTEIN	6%
PROTEIN	5g	VITAMIN A	2%
CARBOHYDRATE	38g	VITAMIN C	*
FAT	23g	THIAMINE	4%
CHOLESTEROL	4mg	RIBOFLAVIN	8%
SODIUM	115mg	NIACIN	8%
POTASSIUM	230mg	CALCIUM	6%
		IRON	6%

*Contains less than 2% of the U.S. RDA of this nutrient.

SATIN FUDGE SAUCE

4 oz. (4 squares) semi-sweet chocolate, chopped
⅓ cup butter or margarine
1½ cups powdered sugar
5-oz. can evaporated milk
1 teaspoon vanilla

In medium heavy saucepan, combine all ingredients except vanilla. Bring mixture to a boil over medium heat, stirring constantly. Reduce heat to low cook 5 minutes, stirring constantly. Remove from heat; stir in vanilla. Serve warm over ice cream or desserts. Cove store in refrigerator. 1⅔ cups.

▣ MICROWAVE DIRECTIONS: In medium microwave-safe bowl, combin all ingredients except vanilla. Microwave on HIGH for 4 to 5 minute or until mixture begins to boil, stirring every 2 minutes. Microwave on DEFROST for 2 to 3 minutes, stirring once. Continue as directed above.

NUTRITION INFORMATION PER SERVING

SERVING SIZE: 1 TABLESPOON		PERCENT U.S. RDA PER SERVING	
CALORIES	70	PROTEIN	*
PROTEIN	1g	VITAMIN A	2%
CARBOHYDRATE	9g	VITAMIN C	*
FAT	4g	THIAMINE	*
CHOLESTEROL	6mg	RIBOFLAVIN	*
SODIUM	30mg	NIACIN	*
POTASSIUM	35mg	CALCIUM	*
		IRON	*

*Contains less than 2% of the U.S. RDA of this nutrient.

This fudge has a wonderfully intense orange flavor highlighted by the crunchy texture of macadamia nuts. Garnish the squares with small pieces of grated orange peel.

MACADAMIA ORANGE FUDGE

2½ cups sugar
½ cup margarine or butter
5-oz. can evaporated milk
7-oz. jar marshmallow creme
12-oz. pkg. (2 cups) semi-sweet
    chocolate chips
3.5-oz. jar macadamia nuts, chopped
2 tablespoons orange-flavored
    liqueur or orange juice
1 tablespoon finely grated
    orange peel

Line 13x9-inch pan with foil so that foil extends over sides of pan; lightly butter foil. In large saucepan, combine sugar, margarine and evaporated milk. Bring to a boil over medium heat, stirring constantly. Boil 5 minutes, stirring constantly; remove from heat. Add marshmallow creme and chocolate chips, stirring until smooth. Stir in macadamia nuts, liqueur and orange peel. Pour into foil-lined pan. Cool to room temperature; score fudge into 36 to 48 squares. Refrigerate until firm. Remove fudge from pan by lifting foil; remove foil from fudge. Using large knife, cut through scored lines. Store in refrigerator. 3 pounds.

MICROWAVE DIRECTIONS: In 2-quart microwave-safe bowl, combine sugar, margarine and evaporated milk. Microwave on HIGH for 6 to 8 minutes or until mixture comes to a full rolling boil, stirring twice during cooking. Add marshmallow creme and chocolate chips. Continue as directed above.

NUTRITION INFORMATION PER SERVING

SERVING SIZE: 1 OUNCE		PERCENT U.S. RDA PER SERVING	
CALORIES	130	PROTEIN	*
PROTEIN	1g	VITAMIN A	*
CARBOHYDRATE	19g	VITAMIN C	*
FAT	6g	THIAMINE	*
CHOLESTEROL	0mg	RIBOFLAVIN	*
SODIUM	30mg	NIACIN	*
POTASSIUM	45mg	CALCIUM	*
		IRON	*

*Contains less than 2% of the U.S. RDA of this nutrient.

Guests will enjoy these perfect after-dinner mints! This recipe makes four dozen candies. Have some tucked away in the freezer for the next time you entertain.

MINT CHOCOLATE STARS

6 oz. chocolate-flavored candy
    coating, cut into pieces
6 oz. (1 cup) milk chocolate chips
¼ cup dairy sour cream, room
    temperature
¼ teaspoon mint extract
12 spearmint leaf gumdrop candies,
    cut into fourths

Line cookie sheets with waxed paper. In small saucepan, melt chocolate-flavored candy coating and milk chocolate chips over low heat, stirring constantly. Remove from heat; whisk in sour cream and mint extract. Fill pastry bag with chocolate mixture and fit with star tip.* Pipe chocolate mixture into 1-inch stars on waxed paper-lined cookie sheets. Garnish top of each candy with spearmint gumdrop piece. Refrigerate until candy is set. 4 dozen candies.

MICROWAVE DIRECTIONS: In medium microwave-safe bowl, combine chocolate-flavored candy coating and milk chocolate chips. Microwave on MEDIUM for 2½ to 3 minutes or until melted, stirring once halfway through cooking. Continue as directed above.

TIP: *Chocolate mixture can be rolled into ¾-inch balls; place on waxed paper-lined cookie sheets. Garnish as directed above.

NUTRITION INFORMATION PER SERVING

SERVING SIZE: 1 CANDY		PERCENT U.S. RDA PER SERVING	
CALORIES	45	PROTEIN	*
PROTEIN	0g	VITAMIN A	*
CARBOHYDRATE	5g	VITAMIN C	*
FAT	3g	THIAMINE	2%
CHOLESTEROL	0mg	RIBOFLAVIN	2%
SODIUM	5mg	NIACIN	*
POTASSIUM	20mg	CALCIUM	*
		IRON	*

*Contains less than 2% of the U.S. RDA of this nutrient.

Make your very own dipped chocolates using vanilla and chocolate-flavored candy coating. These candies store best at room temperature.

DIPPED PEPPERMINT CREAMS

1 lb. vanilla-flavored candy coating, cut into pieces
¼ cup shortening
½ cup finely crushed peppermint candy*

COATING
4 oz. chocolate-flavored candy coating, cut into pieces
1 tablespoon shortening

Line 9x5-inch loaf pan with waxed paper or foil. In medium saucepan, melt vanilla-flavored candy coating and ¼ cup shortening over low heat, stirring constantly. Remove from heat; stir in peppermint candy. Spread mixture into waxed paper-lined pan. Allow candy to stand at room temperature until firm; cut into 1-inch squares. Allow candy to harden completely.

In small saucepan, melt coating ingredients over low heat, stirring constantly. Keep mixture warm. Dip each peppermint candy square halfway into melted coating; allow excess to drip off. Place coating side up on waxed paper. Garnish as desired. Allow to set. Store in single layer at room temperature. 32 candies.

▦ MICROWAVE DIRECTIONS: In medium microwave-safe bowl, combine vanilla-flavored candy coating and ¼ cup shortening. Microwave on MEDIUM for 3 to 5 minutes or until candy is melted; stir until smooth. Stir in crushed peppermint candy. Continue as directed above.

To prepare coating, in medium microwave-safe bowl, combine coating ingredients. Microwave on MEDIUM for 2 to 3 minutes or until melted; stir until smooth. Dip and store candies as directed above.

TIP: *To crush peppermint candy, place candies in plastic bag; secure with twist tie. Crush candies using hammer.

NUTRITION INFORMATION PER SERVING

SERVING SIZE: 1 CANDY		PERCENT U.S. RDA PER SERVING	
CALORIES	130	PROTEIN	*
PROTEIN	1g	VITAMIN A	*
CARBOHYDRATE	11g	VITAMIN C	*
FAT	9g	THIAMINE	10%
CHOLESTEROL	0mg	RIBOFLAVIN	10%
SODIUM	10mg	NIACIN	*
POTASSIUM	30mg	CALCIUM	2%
		IRON	*

*Contains less than 2% of the U.S. RDA of this nutrient.

Include this perfect sweet and salty combination in a gift box of homemade candies.

CANDY-COATED PRETZELS

8 oz. chocolate-flavored or vanilla-flavored candy coating
¼ teaspoon peppermint or mint extract, if desired
4 oz. small twist pretzels
½ cup crushed candy

Melt chocolate-flavored candy coating in medium saucepan over low heat, stirring constantly. Stir in peppermint extract. Keep mixture warm. Dip pretzels into coating; allow excess to drip off. Place on waxed paper. Sprinkle tops of pretzels with crushed candy. 24 pretzels.

▦ MICROWAVE DIRECTIONS: Place candy coating in small microwave-safe bowl. Microwave on HIGH for 1½ to 2 minutes or until smooth, stirring once halfway through cooking. Continue as directed above.

NUTRITION INFORMATION PER SERVING

SERVING SIZE: 1 PRETZEL		PERCENT U.S. RDA PER SERVING	
CALORIES	80	PROTEIN	*
PROTEIN	1g	VITAMIN A	*
CARBOHYDRATE	11g	VITAMIN C	*
FAT	4g	THIAMINE	6%
CHOLESTEROL	0mg	RIBOFLAVIN	6%
SODIUM	85mg	NIACIN	*
POTASSIUM	25mg	CALCIUM	*
		IRON	*

*Contains less than 2% of the U.S. RDA of this nutrient.

Dipped Peppermint Creams

This is a no-cook candy to stir up in a hurry. It makes a perfect little extra treat to pass when dessert is served.

CHOCOLATE CHIP CREAM RUM BALLS

2 (3-oz.) pkg. cream cheese, softened
    4 cups powdered sugar
    1 tablespoon milk
    1 teaspoon rum extract
    ¼ teaspoon cinnamon
    ⅛ teaspoon nutmeg
    ½ cup miniature semi-sweet chocolate chips

GLAZE

    ½ cup miniature semi-sweet chocolate chips
    1 teaspoon oil

Line cookie sheets with waxed paper. In large bowl, beat cream cheese until fluffy. Add 2 cups of the powdered sugar; beat until smooth. Add milk, rum extract, cinnamon and nutmeg; blend well. Gradually add remaining 2 cups powdered sugar. Stir in ½ cup chocolate chips. Refrigerate 1½ hours or until mixture is firm enough to handle. Roll mixture into ¾-inch balls; place on waxed paper-lined cookie sheet.

In small saucepan, melt glaze ingredients over low heat, stirring constantly. Drizzle glaze over candies. Allow glaze to set. Store in single layer in tightly covered container. 5 dozen candies.

NUTRITION INFORMATION PER SERVING

SERVING SIZE: 1 CANDY		PERCENT U.S. RDA PER SERVING	
CALORIES	50	PROTEIN	*
PROTEIN	0g	VITAMIN A	*
CARBOHYDRATE	8g	VITAMIN C	*
FAT	2g	THIAMINE	*
CHOLESTEROL	2mg	RIBOFLAVIN	*
SODIUM	10mg	NIACIN	*
POTASSIUM	15mg	CALCIUM	*
		IRON	*

*Contains less than 2% of the U.S. RDA of this nutrient.

This candy has a unique fudgy texture. It could be packed in a pretty box to give as a special thank you gift.

MILK CHOCOLATE CASHEW DROPS

    ¾ cup firmly packed brown sugar
    ⅓ cup milk
    2 tablespoons light corn syrup
    ½ cup milk chocolate chips
    3 oz. chocolate-flavored candy coating, cut into pieces
    ½ cup chopped salted cashews
    ½ teaspoon vanilla
  36 salted cashew halves

Line cookie sheets with waxed paper. In heavy medium saucepan, combine brown sugar, milk and corn syrup; bring to a boil over medium heat, stirring constantly. Remove from heat. Stir in remaining ingredients except cashew halves; blend well. Refrigerate 15 minutes or until mixture thickens. Drop by scant teaspoonfuls onto waxed paper-lined cookie sheets. Press 1 cashew half on top of each candy. Store in refrigerator. 3 dozen candies.

MICROWAVE DIRECTIONS: In 4-cup microwave-safe measuring cup, combine brown sugar, milk and corn syrup. Microwave on MEDIUM for 4 to 4½ minutes or until mixture boils, stirring once every minute. Stir in remaining ingredients except cashew halves; blend well. Refrigerate 15 minutes or until mixture thickens. Continue as directed above.

NUTRITION INFORMATION PER SERVING

SERVING SIZE: 1 CANDY		PERCENT U.S. RDA PER SERVING	
CALORIES	70	PROTEIN	*
PROTEIN	1g	VITAMIN A	*
CARBOHYDRATE	9g	VITAMIN C	*
FAT	3g	THIAMINE	2%
CHOLESTEROL	0mg	RIBOFLAVIN	2%
SODIUM	5mg	NIACIN	*
POTASSIUM	50mg	CALCIUM	*
		IRON	2%

*Contains less than 2% of the U.S. RDA of this nutrient.

Make this easy fudge using real chocolate chips. Try one of the flavorful variations for a special treat.

THREE IN ONE MICROWAVE MELTAWAY FUDGE

14-oz. can sweetened condensed milk (not evaporated)
12-oz. pkg. semi-sweet chocolate chips
1 teaspoon vanilla

▦ MICROWAVE DIRECTIONS: Line 8-inch square pan with foil so foil extends over sides of pan; butter foil. In 1½-quart microwave-safe bowl or 8-cup microwave-safe measuring cup, combine condensed milk and chocolate chips. Microwave on HIGH for 1½ to 2¾ minutes or until melted, stirring once during cooking. Stir until smooth. Add vanilla; stir well. Pour into foil-lined pan. Refrigerate until set.

Remove fudge from pan by lifting foil; remove foil from fudge. Using large knife, cut fudge into squares. Store in covered container in refrigerator. 1 pound 9 ounces.

CONVENTIONAL DIRECTIONS: Prepare pan as directed above. In medium saucepan, melt condensed milk and chocolate chips over low heat, stirring constantly. Continue as directed above.

Black Forest Fudge: Substitute ¼ teaspoon almond extract for vanilla. Stir ⅔ cup chopped red candied cherries, ½ cup chopped almonds and ½ cup miniature marshmallows into melted chocolate mixture.

Rocky Road Fudge: Stir 1 cup miniature marshmallows and ½ cup chopped nuts into melted chocolate.

NUTRITION INFORMATION PER SERVING
SERVING SIZE: 1 OUNCE		PERCENT U.S. RDA PER SERVING	
CALORIES	150	PROTEIN	2%
PROTEIN	2g	VITAMIN A	*
CARBOHYDRATE	19g	VITAMIN C	*
FAT	7g	THIAMINE	*
CHOLESTEROL	6mg	RIBOFLAVIN	6%
SODIUM	25mg	NIACIN	*
POTASSIUM	125mg	CALCIUM	6%
		IRON	2%

*Contains less than 2% of the U.S. RDA of this nutrient.

Enjoy a taste of the tropics while eating this dark chocolate confection filled with coconut, macadamia nuts and banana chips.

TROPICAL DROP CANDIES

12-oz. pkg. (2 cups) semi-sweet chocolate chips
¾ cup shredded coconut
½ cup chopped macadamia nuts
½ cup chopped banana chips or dried pineapple

Line cookie sheet with waxed paper. Melt chocolate chips in medium saucepan over low heat, stirring constantly. Stir in remaining ingredients; blend well. Drop by teaspoonfuls onto waxed paper-lined cookie sheet. Refrigerate until set, about 30 minutes. Store in airtight container. 24 candies.

▦ MICROWAVE DIRECTIONS: In medium microwave-safe bowl, melt chocolate chips on MEDIUM for 3 to 4 minutes, stirring once halfway through cooking. Stir until smooth. Stir in remaining ingredients; blend well. Continue as directed above.

NUTRITION INFORMATION PER SERVING
SERVING SIZE: 1 CANDY		PERCENT U.S. RDA PER SERVING	
CALORIES	120	PROTEIN	*
PROTEIN	1g	VITAMIN A	*
CARBOHYDRATE	12g	VITAMIN C	*
FAT	8g	THIAMINE	*
CHOLESTEROL	0mg	RIBOFLAVIN	*
SODIUM	0mg	NIACIN	*
POTASSIUM	110mg	CALCIUM	*
		IRON	2%

*Contains less than 2% of the U.S. RDA of this nutrient.

NUTRITION INFORMATION

Pillsbury's NUTRI-CODED system can help you in your daily food planning. Below are guidelines:

SERVING SIZE: This has been determined as a typical serving for each recipe.

CALORIES: The amount of calories a person needs is determined by age, size and activity level. The recommended daily allowances generally are: 1800-2400 for women and children 4 to 10 years of age and 2400-2800 for men.

PROTEIN: The amount of protein needed daily is determined by age and size; the general U.S. RDA is 65 grams for adults and children of at least 4 years of age.

CARBOHYDRATE, FAT, CHOLESTEROL, SODIUM, AND POTASSIUM: Recommended Daily Allowances (RDA) for these nutrients have not been determined; however, the carbohydrate should be adequate so the body does not burn protein for energy. The American Heart Association recommendation for those who wish to restrict dietary cholesterol is for a daily intake that is less than 100 milligrams per 1000 calories and not exceeding a total of 300 milligrams.

PERCENT U.S. RDA PER SERVING: For a nutritionally balanced diet, choose recipes which will provide 100% of the U.S. Recommended Daily Allowance for each nutrient.

Pillsbury Guidelines for Calculating the Nutrition Information:

• When the ingredient listing gives one or more options, the first ingredient listed is the one analyzed.

• When a range is given for an ingredient, the larger amount is analyzed.

• When ingredients are listed as "if desired," these ingredients are included in the nutrition information.

• Serving suggestions listed in the ingredients are calculated in the nutrition information.

• When each bread recipe is analyzed, a serving of yeast-leavened bread is a 1-oz. slice and a quick bread serving is ¹⁄₁₆ of the loaf. Recipes that vary are indicated.

Symbol Meanings:

The following symbols are used in relation to the nutrition data:

   *   Less than 2% of the nutrient
   <1 Less than one gram (or milligram) of the nutrient

Any questions regarding nutrition information in this book should be addressed to:

The Pillsbury Company
Pillsbury Center—Suite 2866
Minneapolis, Minnesota 55402

The primary source for values used in this program is the revised Agriculture Handbook No. 8. The values are only as correct and complete as the information supplied.

NOTE FOR PEOPLE WITH SPECIAL DIETARY NEEDS: CONSULT YOUR PHYSICIAN REGARDING RELIANCE ON THE NUTRITION INFORMATION IN THIS BOOK.
Every effort has been made to ensure the accuracy of this information. However, The Pillsbury Company does not guarantee its suitability for specific medically imposed diets.

INDEX

INDEX

INDEX

*White Chocolate Chunk Brownie
Wedges p. 38*

"DID YOU KNOW THAT YOU DON'T HAVE TO STAND IN LINE TO GET CLASSIC COOKBOOKS?"